CHARIOTS AND HORSES

life lessons from an Olympic rower

jason dorland

HERITAGE

VICTORIA | VANCOUVER | CALGARY

Heritage House Publishing Company Ltd.
www.heritagehouse.ca

LIBRARY AND ARCHIVES CANADA CATALOGUING IN PUBLICATION

Dorland, Jason
    Chariots and horses: life lessons from an Olympic rower / Jason Dorland.

Issued also in an electronic format.
ISBN 978-1-927051-00-9

    1. Dorland, Jason. 2. Rowers—Canada—Biography. 3. Olympics—Participation,
Canadian. 4. Motivation (Psychology). 5. Success. I. Title.

GV790.92.D67A3 2011   797.12'3092   C2011-905027-7

Edited by Melva McLean
Cover design by Jason Dorland
Interior design by Jacqui Thomas
Front cover: Canadian men's eight rowers collapse after finishing last in the
Olympic finals in Seoul in 1988 (COC/The Canadian Press photo); texture image by
Birthe Lunau / iStockphoto.com. *Back cover:* Jason in the coach boat, watching the
Shawnigan Lake Regatta (Nigel Mayes photo).

The author has made every effort to seek permissions from the people named in this
book and the copyright holders of photographs. If any errors or omissions have been made,
please notify the publisher.

The interior of this book was produced on 100% post-consumer
recycled paper, processed chlorine free and printed with
vegetable-based inks.

Heritage House acknowledges the financial support for its publishing program from the
Government of Canada through the Canada Book Fund (CBF), Canada Council for the Arts
and the province of British Columbia through the British Columbia Arts Council and the
Book Publishing Tax Credit.

Canadian Patrimoine
Heritage   canadien

The Canada Council | Le Conseil des Arts
for the Arts | du Canada

BRITISH COLUMBIA
ARTS COUNCIL

14 13 12 11   1 2 3 4

Printed in Canada

DEDICATION AND ACKNOWLEDGEMENTS

This book is dedicated to all of my *teachers*—those who have, with steadfast conviction, patiently stood by me, and tirelessly loved, guided and supported me. Thank you to:

Robyn Meagher and Ike

Mom, Dad, Scott, Wendy and Paul

Neil Campbell

Alex Tay, Alex Zorkin, Stephen Connelly, Max Lang, Travis Walsh, Bart-Jan Caron, Max Wyatt, Sterling Reid, Geoff Roth, Pat Joslyn, James Rogers, Nathan Pocock, Brad Ingham and Jesse Tinker

Bryce Bendickson, Nick Smith, Derek Pattison, Sunny Mehta and David Jones

Darby Berkhout, Dave Walker, Johnny Walker, Kevin O'Brien, Tim Coy and Jamie McKeough

Fiona Taylor

Pat Turner and Trev Neufeld

Peter and Joanne Yates

Doug Weyler

Andrea Stapff

Bryan Donnelly

Rose Dorland and Erik Van Drunen

Wendy Mitchell, Mike Mitchell, Karyn Mitchell, Ian Walker and John Walker

Brian McMahon, John Wallace, Jamie Schafer, Grant Main, Paul Steele, Andy Crosby, Kevin Neufeld and Donnie Telfer

Marius Felix, Tony Carr, Brian Carr and Gary Dukelow

Mike Spracklen, Terry Paul, Al Morrow, Larry Laszlo, Claus Wolter, Jack Nicholson and Jimmy Joy

Holly Eburne, Gillian Sweetland, Fraser MacKay, Peter McCoppin and Katy Lamont

Natalie Spenceley

Jay Connolly, Carol Shaw, Sheila Mahoney and Melva McLean

The publishing team at Heritage House

INTRODUCTION

My experiences as a young boy, teenager and eventually as an elite athlete all embodied the notion that there was one point to competition and that was to beat the living daylights out of your competitors. Maybe it was because I was the last of four children, born into a family that enjoyed and participated in many sports. My dad was a teacher, coach and housemaster at Ridley College, an independent boarding and day school in southern Ontario. My two brothers, my sister and I grew up on a campus that had a pool, two gyms, a rink, squash courts, tennis courts and acres and acres of playing fields and wooded areas. In the summertime we—the "staff brats"—owned it all.

I can't, even for a moment, imagine a better way to have grown up. From morning until the last bit of daylight, we played football, baseball, tennis, squash, swimming, hide and seek. You name it, we probably played it. Even at night, once we were old enough, we played flashlight tag. We were active, healthy and too busy to get into trouble. My siblings were significantly older than I was. Emotionally and physically, they were always way ahead of me in their development. When you're six and your next-oldest brother is eleven, your sister is thirteen, and your oldest brother is sixteen, you are at a considerable disadvantage when it comes to competition.

As I grew older, I got bigger but I certainly never caught up. They were always bigger and stronger.

It's important for you to know that my parents never pushed me or my siblings to get involved with or stay in sports. Sometimes I wish they had taken a greater interest in my sports. I think it was just two parents trying to stay impartial and not come across as being any more excited about one child's success versus another's.

As a teenager and young man growing up in St. Catharines, Ontario, our dad had been a bit of a jock. In fact, before the Second World War, the Chicago White Sox had scouted him as a pitcher. After the war he enrolled at McGill University, where he studied physical education. He played on numerous varsity teams, everything from basketball and baseball to boxing and wrestling—he was a varsity champion. After the war he followed his father before him and joined the St. Catharines rowing club and won a Canadian Henley Championship as a lightweight.

The sportsmanship code that Dad had grown up with, and the one that Ridley used as its motto for its sports program, was, "If you lose, say nothing. If you win, say less." That philosophy, which continues today, began with the Ridley's first headmaster, Dr. Harry Griffith. At any rate, it worked for Dad and we were constantly reminded of its value. It just didn't always apply when siblings were involved. In fact, if us boys got too rowdy, he would deliver his standard, "Gosh, boys. Cut it out!"

You see, my brothers, Scott and Paul, saw everything between them as a competition, and most of the time it wasn't friendly. They certainly never came to blows, but you could tell they took every game seriously, with each of them striving for the bragging rights that came with winning. Several times the bragging turned into one-upping banter, and my sister, Wendy, the peacemaker, would often chime in and tell them to "cool it," but she was just as competitive. She was strong, athletic and liked taking it to her brothers any chance she could get.

My oldest brother, Scott, was always organizing events, which involved everything from Ping-Pong tournaments to hockey games to croquet matches. Yes, croquet—only with special rules. We called it "Killer Croquet." The course was laid out over an enormous expanse of land and, instead of the usual polite tap that you sometimes dealt your competition, you were encouraged to bash the crap out of each other's balls. There was nothing polite and proper about Killer Croquet. It was all-out war, and I usually got killed.

In fact, no matter what the game or event, I came out the loser. After many of our competitions I would go to my room in a rage and crawl under my bed and cry. I wasn't mad at my brothers; I was pissed off at myself. I used to tell myself, "You have to try harder. You have to find a way to win."

I was always good at keeping my emotions to myself, but on the odd occasion when my brothers would ease off during games or races and let me win, I would lose my temper. I wasn't a charity case and I didn't want, nor did I think I needed, their help. I understood that they were doing it to be nice, but I hated it. "Stop it!" I would yell. "I don't want to win that way!"

Along with the homegrown tournaments and pickup games, all four of us were also involved in organized sports. We belonged to sports leagues and clubs outside of our school teams. We all swam for the St. Catharines Swim Club. Scott and Wendy were both excellent swimmers and won countless races and titles. By the time I had joined, I had a name to live up to. Even though my siblings were long gone from the pools, I was still competing against them. I wore the pressure of those expectations all of the time. It didn't come from them or from my parents. It was never discussed at home or in the car going to and from meets. It was just something that I had created.

I loved training. Life was great when swimming meant I could just focus on pushing myself during practice. But come race day, I was a wreck. I would get so nervous, I felt sick all day long. The thought of not winning was unbearable. I would sooner not race than lose. At one large regional championship meet, I hid in a locker in the change room just before my race was called, and I stayed in there, waiting until it was over. To this day, I still get nervous when I walk into a sports complex and I smell a pool.

Basically, I'm a terrible loser. I always have been—from my youth, through my high school racing, through my Olympic experience and my coaching. Even though as a coach it's been my job to ensure that I role-model a cool-headed, composed and professional individual who strives to teach his athletes that there is more to life than winning, inside I have struggled all my life to understand what exactly that is.

For as long as I could remember, winning was the goal of every race. The first time I saw the impact of winning was in a running race against my Grade 2 teacher, Mrs. Hawkins. One afternoon our class was engaged in running races and I had won all of mine. Someone yelled out, "You race Jason, Mrs. Hawkins." The rest of the students joined in and coerced her into racing me. I won. The other students were so impressed that I had run faster than our teacher.

"Wow, you beat Mrs. Hawkins. You're fast," someone said.

I can still remember how important I felt. I believed I had just done something special, and that feeling stayed with me so strongly and so long that it created demons with which I have done battle over and over again.

This story is about fighting those demons, about how they got inside my head and about how, with the help of some amazing people—one in particular—I have learned to keep them at bay. Along the way I have become a better competitor, a better coach and, ultimately, a better person. I hope that by sharing my story, you may continue to develop a greater appreciation for and greater understanding of the reality that there is more to sport, to business and to life, than just winning.

JASON DORLAND

ST. CATHARINES, ONTARIO, 2011

1 ▬▶———•———

THE SEOUL OLYMPICS

Travelling to Seoul was an exhausting trip that crossed seven time zones. The general rule is that you need one day of recovery for every time zone, so we arrived two weeks early. With regularly scheduled meals and daily exercise, we quickly acclimatized ourselves to the local time and weather, and became familiar with the rowing venue.

Colourful flags from all of the participating countries welcomed visitors at the entrance to the site. The rowing course itself was like a huge outdoor swimming pool. Evenly spaced white buoys precisely marked the lanes, and brilliant red, blue and yellow banners lined the water's edge. Massive billboards displayed the Olympic Games mascots, Hodori and Hosuni—male and female stylized tigers—for the television audience at home.

Being ready for the first heat of a competition involves tapering (reducing training in the days leading up to competition) just enough to be strong but not overworked. After our training subsided, we found ourselves eagerly awaiting the start of the Games.

The price for an athlete to attend the opening ceremonies of an Olympics is spending hours on your feet outside the stadium waiting for things to start. Some competitors whose events run early often choose not to attend the opening. Our rowing event wouldn't start until the Games were well underway, so the entire crew attended, each of us carrying two Frisbees.

We were surrounded by athletes from all over the world. I, a young man from St. Catharines, Canada, could never have imagined it, yet, there I was, part of the greatest competition on earth. Awed by it all, my obsession with winning a gold medal lifted long enough for me to appreciate how just getting there was an amazing feat in and of itself.

Then I became aware of the size of some of the athletes. The Europeans were especially impressive: their height and musculature were awesome. I kept telling myself that it didn't matter. The 1984 Canadian Olympic men's eight (a shell with eight rowers) in Los Angeles had been the smallest crew in the final, and they had won.

As we waited patiently in the late afternoon sun, some countries showed off their team cheers. We Canadians, being more restrained, intended to show our pride by throwing our two Frisbees into the crowd once we entered the stadium. Although most team cheers got a good laugh or applause, "U-S-A, U-S-A" was drowned out by the surrounding booing. As a young boy, I would have been scolded for booing competitors. That one gesture reminded me these were the Olympics—no holds were barred here.

Finally, after hours of waiting, it was our turn to walk through the darkness of the tunnel and into the blinding lights of the stadium. The enormous crowd was on its feet cheering. The sound was deafening. I could feel the electricity in the night air. Tingles ran up my spine and goosebumps appeared on my arms. I felt giddy with excitement, just like a kid on Christmas morning. I threw my Frisbees as hard as I could and watched them disappear into the lights.

As the Olympic flag was carried into the stadium by eight Korean Olympic medallists, I couldn't see for the tears flooding my eyes. I thought of my parents and of all they had sacrificed—their time and their money—to support my Olympic dream. I noticed that our five-man, Paul Steele, had tears in his eyes too. The "Man of Steele," as we called him, my mentor in the boat, was as emotional as I was. For some reason I had assumed he would take all of this in stride. He had been to the Los Angeles Olympics in 1984 and had won a gold medal. The fact that he was emotional made me less self-conscious about showing my feelings.

One of the final torchbearers, Sohn Kee-chung, a 1936 Olympic gold medallist and Korean national hero, entered the stadium and passed the torch to Lim Chun-ae, the final Olympic torchbearer and star of the 10th Asian Games. She made her way, through a sea of athletes trying to snap her picture, to the platform at the base of the Olympic cauldron. The audience and athletes watched in silence as the platform slowly rose to the lip of the caldron. With doves flying around the stadium, the cauldron was lit, and the silence was broken with cheers and applause. What a show!

The next day, our work began.

Neil Campbell was our coach or, as we liked to think of him, the 10th member of the crew. Amazingly, he hadn't started rowing until he was in his late twenties and, at the age of 34, competed for Canada in the 1964 Olympic Games in Japan. Four years later, he stroked the Canadian men's eight in the Olympic Games in Mexico—not because they couldn't find anyone else for that coveted seat, but because he was that good.

I first met Neil when I was a six-year-old kid at Ridley. My dad was manager of the rowing team by then, and Neil Campbell was the head coach. It was natural for the two of them to become friends.

One evening in the summer of 1972, my parents went out for dinner with the Campbells and invited them back to our place after the meal.

"Jason, this is Mr. Campbell," my mom said.

My little hand disappeared into his, but I squeezed as hard as I could and said, "Nice to meet you, Mr. Campbell."

"Nice to meet you, too, Jason. You can call me Neil," he replied with a wink and warm smile. "You gonna row for me someday like your brother?"

Without any hesitation, I said, "Yup. I've already started exercising. Wanna see?"

I ran to get the seven-pound dumbbell that my dad had given me and began going through my workout regimen, most of which I made up on the spot.

Neil didn't seem to mind. He just kept nodding and smiling and offering the occasional, "Oh, that's a good one. You should do lots of those." A couple of times he said, "I don't think I would do too many of those. They look like they could mess you up." And so it went for about 20 minutes with me, in my blue summer pajamas, demonstrating the finer details of rowing land training to a man who would become an international coaching legend.

When Neil began his coaching career at Ridley College in the late 1960s, he asked Lloyd Percival, a sports scientist in Toronto, to put together land and water training workouts. Neil wanted to replicate on land not only the rowing motion but also the overall physical challenges associated with the sport. From December to March his athletes endured four land-based phases of weight training. He pushed hard to help crews discover exactly what they were capable of achieving, and when he asked his crews to do something, he would always prove that he could do it first.

When it came my time to be coached by him in the early 1980s, I found his notion of "leading from the front" tremendously reassuring. I knew that he understood what we were going through because he had lived it. He would do exercises with us and often last longer than we did. During weight training, Neil would get us to lie face down on a two-inch by ten-inch plank of wood that was long enough to straddle two wooden sawhorses. The exercise was to pull a bar with weights up to hit the bench as many times as we could without dropping it. When we let go or didn't hit the bench two times in a row, we were done—our teenage bodies exhausted. Then Neil, our fiftysomething coach, would climb onto the bench and grab hold of the 80-pound bar. We would watch, listening to the rhythmic clank, once every three seconds until the bar literally fell out of his hands, and that was usually somewhere well over 200 repetitions. He was constantly challenging himself the way he expected us to challenge ourselves. We were impressed. As were others. So much so, that in 1981 Neil was awarded the Order of Canada for his coaching and mentoring of young athletes.

My first year doing these phases with Neil, I learned something about myself that still serves me 30 years later. Working with a 70- or 80-pound bar, we did 10 repetitions of 7 different exercises as many times as we could in 20 minutes. Neil made it a race—everything was competition with Neil—with the winner the one who scored the highest number of repetitions in 20 minutes.

One day I was about 10 minutes into the session and on track to get a decent score. I finished a set, put the bar down, and bent over, gasping for enough air to keep continuing the session. Neil saw me, got up from his own workout and came over. Standing right in front me he said, in a strong, but calm, voice, "Pick it up. You're not tired. Come on, Jase, keep going."

I grabbed the 70-pound bar and continued with the next exercise. When I finished, I put down the weight, heaving with exhaustion, trying desperately to recover. My head was spinning from the nausea, and my legs, back and arms were searing with pain. I was done—at least I thought I was.

"What are you doing? Pick up the bar. Keep going. You're not tired yet," Neil said.

I looked at him sweat dripping from my brow and thought, *He's gotta be crazy. I can't pick this thing up again.*

Then in a stern voice he said, "Pick up the bar and keep going. You're done when you fall over."

I bent down and picked up the bar. When the 20 minutes was up I had achieved my best score ever. Trying desperately to breathe, my lungs burning, my body wobbling back and forth, I bent over, my arms barely managing to brace against my rubbery legs. Neil leaned down, squeezed the back of my neck and quietly said, "Don't you ever forget this day."

What Neil did in those 10 minutes was to help me redefine something we all possess—human potential. From that day forward, my life changed; everything became a new challenge. Rowing training, and redefining my perceptions of my limitations there, became a new experience, a thrill. The results were addictive. As I started winning more, I saw that the possibilities were up to me, that I controlled the pace and the arrival of the finish line. I came to the realization that I was capable of winning anything if I believed it was possible.

The opportunity to row for Neil in the Olympics brought with it the confidence that I had felt when I'd rowed for him as a young teenager. It was like having the toughest older brother on the block. Nobody messed with you and that was comforting.

Life as a rower in an Olympic village is simple: wake up, eat breakfast, travel to the course by bus, row, return to the village by bus, eat lunch, nap, travel back to the course, row, return to the village, eat dinner, play cards and then go to bed. It was a routine that we were used to and embraced fully knowing it was the best way to show up on race day ready to go. It also afforded us the necessary time to get used to our new boat.

We were rowing a brand new shell that had been designed by a young boat builder from the United States named Mike Vespoli.

Empacher boats were pretty much the standard, but Mike's design for the US men's eight garnered world attention when the team won the 1987 World Championships in Copenhagen. Mike had designed a boat that was supposed to better his 1987 model, but, for some reason, the US Olympic team chose to row the older model in Seoul.

When we were in the final stages of our training in Canada, Neil agreed to try out Mike's new design and compare it with our Empacher. We did a series of 500-metre pieces (a set time or distance that is generally rowed at race pace) in both boats. The times showed that Mike's boat was faster. We also preferred the feel of the boat, the way it cut through water and provided a more stable platform for racing. Neil gave Mike a dollar to make it official, and from that day forward Mike's boat was our new chariot.

The team itself was also new. Andy Crosby, our four-man, Jamie Schaefer, our seven-man, and I, the three-man, were the three youngest horses. We referred to ourselves as "The Young Guns" because we had the highest ergometer scores (used to measure power and fitness) in Canada. What we lacked in experience, we made up for in enthusiasm and strength.

The two other new horses were the bookends—Donnie Telfer in the bowseat (the rower closest to the front, or bow, of a multi-rower shell) and John Wallace at stroke (the rower in the stern responsible for the stroke rate and rhythm). They were both accomplished rowers; they had excellent technique, good power-to-weight ratios and they brought the right sort of chemistry to our boat.

The remaining three horses were Kevin Neufeld in two-seat, Paul Steele, our five-man, and Grant Main, our six-man. All three of them had been part of the 1984 Olympic gold medal crew, as had our coxie (responsible for steering and race strategy), Brian McMahon.

As a high school athlete at Ridley, I knew of them only because Neil coached the Canadian national team during the summer months and sometimes he would share stories of their skill and accomplishments. When I first started attending national team rowing camps and competing against them, I had to forget that these guys were my teenage heroes. I realized that I couldn't continue to idolize them and row with them at the same time; I had to believe that I deserved to be in the same boat as them.

The Russians, the Brits and the Italians were our main competition in the first heat. The winner of the heat would advance straight to the final. The remaining teams would race in a repechage, or rep, the French word for second chance. Though no one in our crew was in the habit of racing for second place, given our lack of experience as a team—we hadn't competed together as a crew except at the Lucerne Regatta two months earlier, where we had placed fourth—a repechage wouldn't necessarily be a bad thing; in fact, it would be an added race to gain more experience.

Before a race begins, the starting judge must ensure that each of the crews is lined up straight and ready to go. He addresses each crew, in French, by their country's name followed by, *"Prêt* (ready)?" If a crew is ready, the coxie leaves his hand down; if not, he raises it. When all of the boats are ready, the starter says, "Attention!" Then, after a definite pause, a beep sounds to start the race.

These moments before the start are nerve-wracking. Except for the sound of the starting judge asking if coxies are ready and the coxies asking crewmembers to *"touch it up"* (take a small stroke to realign their course), all is silent. Now and again, some rowers scream and yell at the start of a race to intimidate competitors. Those crews generally don't win and just end up looking even more ridiculous. Most rowers try to relax and prepare for the race, and each rower has his own process.

My process was to approach each racecourse as if it were a battlefield, each race as if it were a war and each competitor as if he were an enemy. I would look over at each of the rowers sitting in the same seat as me and think, *There is no way any of you guys are going to race harder than I am. I'm prepared to do whatever it takes to beat you.* By the time a race began I would have built up a good dose of hatred toward all of my competitors and I would be burning inside to get on with it.

"Attention!"

BEEP.

We were off.

Thirty strokes into the race and any thoughts of the rep were gone. Lengthening out to 38 strokes per minute, we were almost a length up on the entire field and gunning for more, but as 750 metres approached, our initial speed had faded, and the Russian and British crews had not only regained the distance we had opened up, they were passing us. Our impressive start had given us a quick lead, but our inexperience racing as a crew was beginning to show. We struggled through the last half of the race but mounted a late charge to finish second to the Russians.

In some races everything connects: the boat feels light, and it's as if you just can't pull hard enough. You shoot for those races and when you hit them, it's a feeling all its own. When everything aligns, when all of the pushing, pulling, heaving and squeezing, when the power of each rower is contributing to the boat's speed, the synergy of motion is unequalled in any other sport.

In other races, nothing connects: the boat feels heavy, and no matter how hard you pull, it doesn't seem to move. Racing full-out and not seeing a return for the effort is exhausting. More than that, the marriage of the physical and emotional pain of losing is a crappy feeling.

The Russians and the West Germans, who had won their heat, advanced to the final, leaving those of us remaining to battle it out two days later in two repechages. The boats placing first and second in each rep would fill the remaining four lanes in the final.

We drew the United States, Italy and Korea in our rep. That meant we would have to win or at least beat either the Americans or the Italians, while the Aussies, the Brits and the Japanese would battle for the other two lanes in the second rep.

The next day in practice we focused on lengthening into a better racing rate after our explosive start. There wasn't much point in getting out in front of our competition if we couldn't build on it. I was certain we could pull it off. Getting one more 2,000-metre piece under our belts would set us up perfectly for the final. By then, we would have worked out all of the kinks and be ready to have the race of our lives, and, more importantly, win Olympic gold.

On rep day, after a decent warm-up, we sat ready, waiting for the starter's command.

"Canada, *prêt?* Italie, *prêt?* États-Unis, *prêt?* Corée du Sud, *prêt?* Attention!"

BEEP.

Twenty strokes into the race we found ourselves nowhere near the front. We hadn't taken off like a rocket the way we had in the heat. In fact, the US boat was out front and the Italians were right there with us. Command after command from our coxie garnered nothing. All through the first 500 metres we heard his trademark growl reminding us to hit the water together. "Catch! Legs! Squeeze!" He had been under the gun before and in situations similar to or worse than this one, and if anyone knew how to pull this crew together and fix this mess, he could.

At the 1,000-metre mark, the severity of the situation hit home to him. "Okay boys, we're down to the Yanks. The Italians are up as well. It's now or never. Here we go. The stern four with catches. The bow four with finishes in two strokes. One, breathe! Two, breathe! Go!"

Three strokes into that piece it felt like someone was trying to rock the boat back and forth. We were spinning our wheels even more. With 900 metres to go—less than two minutes and 45 seconds remaining in the race—it looked like the defending Olympic champions weren't going to advance to the final, weren't going to be able to defend their title.

"No! It's not working. No!" yelled out our stroke, John Wallace.

If the boat felt brutal where I was sitting in three-seat, it must have felt even worse for John. Being at the stern of the boat, he could feel every little imperfection coming from the guys behind. With 500 metres and less than a minute and a half to go, we were still down. The Americans still had close to a boat length of open water on us—that was equivalent to six seconds on the clock. The Italians had almost a boat length on us as well—that was equivalent to three seconds. If things didn't change quickly, we were done.

That was when Kevin Neufeld, sitting directly behind me, let out a cry of desperation. Kevin wasn't very tall but he had enormous musculature. He was a boat mover. I once rowed behind him, and at the end of each stroke his powerful finish was like a wall of muscle closing in on me.

"Come on! Let's go!"

His voice travelled down the boat like an axe, instantly cutting through all the noise and chatter of the boats beside us. I had never seen Kevin mad, but as his words sailed by me I could feel the rage that had created them. He had been there in Los Angeles in 1984 and wasn't about to let this race go without a fight.

The effect of his battle cry was immediate. On the next stroke we came together and moved back on the leaders. On the next, we moved again. I could feel the boat go faster with each stroke. It was infectious, each guy trying to throw whatever he could into the fire that was generating this newfound speed. We had hit one of those moments where you couldn't pull hard enough. No matter how fast we jammed our legs down, heaved our backs and shoulders and squeezed our arms, the boat just kept getting lighter. I had been in crews that could shift gears in the last 500 metres but never like this.

"Yeah, that's it. Open 'er up, Johnny! Here we go, boys, we're movin' now. Come on! Come on! Right through these Italians."

You could hear the confidence in Brian's voice. With 200 metres to go we had passed the Italians and were closing in on the Americans. Brian called for another rate jump, with legs and catches, and he got it. As we broke into the last 100 metres of the race, we were sitting one boat length up on the Italians and closing fast on the Americans. When the finish horn sounded, we sat second to the Americans. We had done it! We had saved ourselves from disaster. We could now claim as ours one of the two outside lanes of the 1988 Olympic final for the men's eight.

As we turned and went for our recovery row, the boat was silent. We had made the final, but the pain the effort had cost was beyond words. We had all gone well into our tanks in a big way to find that kind of a finish. You don't do that sort of thing for free. Our bodies would take some time to recover, and we all knew they only had two days to do that.

The emotional discomfort was just as bad. Yes, we had qualified, but we had done it with a Hail Mary, last-ditch effort. This time we had completely pooched the first half of the race and saved it in the second. We hadn't rowed a perfect race yet and we had only one chance left.

When I was 16, in Grade 11 and rowing in the heavyweight eight race at the Stotesbury Cup Regatta in Philadelphia for the first time, we came second in the final. It was our first real race as a crew, having only solidified the lineup weeks earlier. After the race, one of the guys took out his silver medal and said, "The next one's going to be gold." Neil was within earshot. He turned and looked at us with fiery eyes, came storming over and said, "This one should've been fucking gold! This one!" We stood frozen, too afraid to move or say anything.

That day in Seoul, Neil was waiting for us back at the dock, in his classic stance—a bit hunched, eyes squinting with his arms hanging at his sides, lifeless. I grabbed my oar and began to stagger up to the pavilion where our boat was stored. My legs were wobbly, my arms exhausted and my lungs angry. With my legs cursing each step, I noticed two very large bodies standing directly in my path closer to the pavilion. I changed course just a bit, but the two bodies moved with me so I forced myself to stand a little taller and show no pain. I was thinking, *Don't look tired.* Neil had told us at Ridley, "Always make it look like you could turn around and go do it again. Even though it would probably kill ya."

As I got closer, I looked up and saw that they were two members of the Russian eight. They looked at me, nodded their heads and said, "Good race."

They smiled; I returned the smile, acknowledged the compliment. Then I thought, *Did I hear that right?* Those were two of the Russians I would be racing in the final. The Russians never have much to do with any of the other athletes, especially before a race but these two had obviously been struck by what we had accomplished. To me that was saying something.

What we had just achieved finally began to sink in. At the international level in the men's eight, crews might win by a second or two but rarely by more than five or six seconds. Boats just don't move that much on other boats over a 2,000-metre course, which should take anywhere from five and a half to six minutes. To have a boat open up a seven-second lead in the first 1,000 metres was impressive and unusual. To have a boat take back six to seven seconds over the last 500 metres was extraordinary, essentially unheard of. Later I learned that the Australian coach had told his crew they had to break away from us early in the final if they were to stand a chance of winning. He had said, "If the Canadians are anywhere in contention with 500 metres to go with that sort of speed, the race will be over."

The day before the final we went for a morning row. After a couple of trips along the course, with some starts and transition pieces, we came off the water feeling ready. We had a brief talk as a crew. There really wasn't much to say; we all knew exactly what we had to do. All that was left was to do it.

For no other reason than to keep ourselves busy, we gave the boat a quick wash while Neil joked around trying to keep the mood upbeat. Our gristly, fierce and sometimes intimidating coach could be very playful at times. With our chariot clean and put away, we quickly ran upstairs to the second floor of the pavilion to watch the final for the men's 100-metre dash. Ben Johnson was going head-to-head with Carl Lewis to see who could claim the title of "World's Fastest Man."

A tidal wave of solid muscle rolled forward as all eight sprinters began their quest for the finish line. After a few strides, Ben Johnson had a slight lead on the rest of the group, his enormous legs driving harder and faster with each stride. Then, just when it looked like he was at his top speed, he appeared to find another gear. He was all alone at the finish line, not only the fastest man but an Olympic and World Record holder with a crazy fast time of 9.79 seconds.

I got up and headed for the stairs, excited that Johnson had won so convincingly. Donnie Telfer was beside me as we made our way down the stairs. He leaned toward me and quietly said, "Now it's our turn."

I smiled and said, "You're damn right."

The rest of the day was filled with eating, napping, playing cards, while Led Zeppelin and Rush played in the background. All of us, including Neil, were housed together in the Olympic Village, in something like a large condo, although not quite as fancy by North American standards.

At bedtime, Neil made his rounds as he did every night to say goodnight. When he got to my room, he knocked on the open door and came in. Andy Crosby, my roommate, was in the washroom. Neil came over to my bed and sat down beside me.

"How're you doing, Jase?"

"Good. I'm ready to go," I answered.

"You should be," replied Neil. Then he reached up and put his hand on the back of my neck. Neil had huge hands. They were strong and leathery but always warm. He squeezed my neck like he always did when he wanted me to know that he was there for me and said, "Hey, Jase. Do you remember that time when you were a little boy and you showed me all of those exercises with that little barbell and told me you were going to row for me some day?"

I looked up at him in complete shock. Lost in his warm eyes, I couldn't speak. I didn't think he'd remembered that day.

He smiled and said, "Who'd have thunk?" He got up and walked to the door, turned and said, "Have a good sleep. We're going to war tomorrow."

I was struck by what had just happened. In every way it represented the brilliance that was Neil Campbell. In every sense of the word he was an athlete's coach. What he knew, he knew because he had lived it, figured it out through trial and error. He didn't coach from a psychology textbook or from some coaching clinic handout—he coached from his heart.

In all the years he'd known me he had never referred to that night when, at the age of six, I'd done all those stupid exercises for him. Instead, he had waited more than 15 years for the perfect moment and he hadn't said too much, just enough—"Who'd have thunk?" Just enough to get me thinking, "Okay, Jase, here you are. You've made it to the Olympic final. Now what are you going to do about it?" I lay back in bed, with tears streaming down my cheeks. It was like I was six years old again. I awoke the next morning after a good night's sleep and immediately thought to myself, *This is it. This is the day I win my Olympic gold.* I was as ready as I'd ever be.

I've always loved the morning row on the day of a final. It gives you a chance to get your blood flowing, to get your muscles stretched out and go over some final race strategies with the team. That morning, we had a good row. The boat felt light. The stroke rates (or number of strokes executed per minute) came easily. We were ready. There was nothing left to do except race. About 45 minutes before the final, we all went into a locker room to have a quick meeting. Neil wasn't big on pre-race talks. He figured if you didn't know what you were supposed to do by this point, then you were in a whole lot more trouble than a 10-minute meeting could ever solve. He simply said, "Go out there and do what you're capable of. Come out of the gates the way you can and then lengthen into a strong racing rate and go to work. Then, when it's time to go—well, you all know what to do."

I could tell from the tone of Brian's voice that he too felt at ease. Brian had been coxing Neil's crews for over 10 years. He too had gone to Ridley and coxed some of the fastest crews the school had ever seen. He had backed into enough starting gates during his career to have faced almost any situation you could imagine. I was glad to know he was up there calling the shots. He had done it in Los Angeles, and I expected he would help us do it again today.

As we sat in our lane, locked in, with the boat holder waiting for the starter to begin aligning the crews, I began my usual pre-race routine. I looked over at the three-man of each crew and thought, *Well this is it. This is my race, and to hell with you.* The anger I built up that day was stronger than anything I had mustered before. I wanted to win more than anything and I was willing to go anywhere in my mind to do it.

Finally, the starter's voice broke the palpable silence that gripped all of the waiting participants. Like everyone, I thought, *This is it— it's time,* but instead of starting to align us, the starter announced that the West Germans had broken some equipment during their warm-up and that he had to ask each team if it was okay to postpone the race by 15 minutes. He added that if one country objected, the

West Germans would be disqualified, and the race would continue at the scheduled time.

Each country agreed that it was okay to postpone the race—not one objected. The next day the press would write about how that one act embodied the true spirit of the Olympics, and that if it had been any other sport, the West Germans would have been done.

As far as I was concerned, why would you say no? Why would you want to be deemed the winner without beating all of your competitors on the day? Where was the satisfaction in winning a race if you had won on a technicality? There would forever be people who would say, "Oh yeah, but the West Germans weren't there."

Our boat holder released us and we rowed off down the course at a firm paddle. Once we were away from the others, we stopped and did some more starts and a few 10-stroke pieces to keep warm. We couldn't believe it; a perfect warm-up, perfect conditions—a slight tailwind—and now we had to wait. You could feel the tension come into the boat as we finished each piece, stopped and then discussed how many more we should do. Each guy in the boat had been at the peak of his emotional readiness, bursting to go, and now we were all coming down off that high in a way that none of us were used to or, for that matter, knew how to.

When the West Germans were ready, all of the countries headed back to the starting area and manoeuvred into position. Everything seemed back to normal, but I could tell something had changed. The electricity we had all felt moments ago was gone. While we sat, once again, waiting for the starter, I could hear Brian telling John that he wanted to false start on purpose.

"We're flat. We've gotta rev things up, Johnny."

Brian was right, an intentional false start would allow us to blast out of the gates one more time before being called back, but it also meant risking disqualification if we false started again.

I thought it was a great idea. The rush of six boats pounding out of the gates was just the thing we needed to recharge the air. Then, someone else up front said, "No. Don't do it! Don't do it, Brian!"

"Australie, *prêt?*"

"États-Unis, *prêt?*"

I didn't dare speak up—it wasn't my place. I was just a 24-year-old kid in a boat of Olympic champions. There were a few more abrupt exchanges and it was decided—we would not false start.

"Allemange de l'Ouest, *prêt?*"

Sitting ready, once again, I thought, *Here it is, Jase. Here's your dream—go get it!* As the starter continued aligning each country, I could feel myself focus in.

"Russie, *prêt?*"

"Grande-Bretagne, *prêt?*"

"Canada, *prêt?*"

Brian offered, in his quiet voice, "Here we go, boys. This is it. Breathe. Breathe."

"Attention!"

BEEP.

My hands squeezed the oar, fighting to bear the weight of the first stroke. When you push against over 1,000 pounds of dead weight, it's heavy. When you have seven other guys doing it with you, it's lighter. This was heavy. We came out of the blocks and hit our rates, but we didn't hit our top speed. Where was the start we had produced in this same lane only 15 minutes earlier? As for me, I had rallied the hatred, but it wasn't as good as it had been before the delay.

We ploughed through our first 20 strokes, heavy and sluggish but we were still up with the field. It was an uninspiring start but at the 250-metre mark, we were tied for the lead with the West Germans. Brian barked at us non-stop, instructing piece after piece, call after call, yet we could not shift our stride or our speed.

Then, the Brits right beside us started to move back on our lead. Stroke after stroke, they took one seat after another. Usually when one boat starts to move on another, the other senses it and responds, but we had nothing. Our boat got heavier and heavier. I wanted to yell something like Kevin had in our repechage but, again, I caught myself. It wasn't my place in this boat. At Ridley, I would have yelled out for us to fight back. That day, I remained silent.

At the 1,000-metre mark we were in fifth place and fading. We were having the worst race, possibly the worst row, we'd ever had. Brian, still trying to sound positive, searching through his years of experience for a command that could snap us out of this fog, decided on a final frantic plea, "Kevin, Paul, Grant! One more time, here we go! On this one! Now!" To me it sounded like a final attempt to rally what the four of them had done four years earlier in Los Angeles. This time there was nothing. The race was all but over.

BEEP.

The first horn blast came, indicating that someone other than us had crossed the line.

BEEP.

Then another.

BEEP.

And another.

Each blast of the horn was like a physical blow until we finally struggled across the line, placing sixth. Not only had we lost, we had come dead last. No one said a word. We all sat there, disheartened, floating dead in the water.

Head down, bent over my oar, I couldn't have felt any worse. My lungs burned as though a lit torch had just been shoved down my throat, searing everything it touched. My ears rang at a high pitch. My vision was blurred from pulses surging in from the sides of my eyes. The lactic acid in my legs and arms rendered movement impossible. It filled my limbs, stretching my skin until it felt like my entire body was preparing to tear open just to relieve the pressure. The nausea and dizziness was consuming and unrelenting, growing stronger and stronger with every passing minute.

Reality began to sink in. I had lost my race, the one race that I had been dreaming of since I was a kid. How had I let that happen? I felt empty, alone and badly beaten. I wanted the boat to fill up with water and sink. The ringing in my ears was soon replaced with the sounds of cheering coming from the West German boat. I looked over and saw them celebrating. In an instant I was enraged. I wanted to strike out at them. There was no gracious moment of a sportsmanlike acceptance of defeat. *Well rowed, Germany*. Bullshit. I was furious at them. They had stolen my medal. They had taken away my race—my dream.

We started off on a cool-down row, until someone said, "Let's just go in, Brian."

What was the point anyway? We were done. We had rowed our last race and we were finished. We rowed the boat into the dock where Neil grabbed Donnie's oar and pulled us in without a word. There was nothing to be said, no words that could ease the frustration of not rowing to our potential. It was one thing to lose to a crew that was just that much faster than you and quite another thing to get destroyed by someone you had previously beaten. That was the kicker. The pill that was impossible to swallow. The one that would for years to come get stuck in my throat every time I thought about the race.

The remaining week in Seoul was like a bad hangover—a fog that never lifted. Everyone seemed numb. Neil flew home to Canada right away. He had a business and a wife to get back to. Days after his "perfect" race, Ben Johnson was busted for steroid use and had to surrender his gold medal. Canadian athletes were instructed not to talk to the media and advised not to wear our Canadian team outfits downtown because the Canadian Olympic Committee wasn't sure how the Korean public might react to a Canadian's shameful act at their Olympic Games. To me, the scandal added insult to injury.

When the closing ceremonies finally arrived, I marched into the Olympic Stadium feeling like a spectator. I was no longer part of a team; our rowing crew had pretty much disbanded. Although many of us had spent time together during the week following our final, we never discussed our race or what, if anything, had gone so horribly wrong. At the time it didn't strike me as strange. We didn't have an answer and we didn't want to relive the moment.

At the closing ceremonies, screaming fans were there just as they had been two weeks prior, waving flags and cheering. Bright lights and loud music again dazzled the senses, but the energy I had felt—the buzz that was so electric I could feel it in my veins— was now gone. I was no longer filled with national pride. There were no tears of joy; no thoughts of family or friends. There was just an empty ache inside that I was trying to ignore. Even with the prevailing winds, the flight home was painfully long. We landed in Vancouver and, after saying goodbye to the athletes from the West Coast, I caught a flight to Toronto and drove to St. Catharines. There, the reunion with my family—Mom, Dad, my middle brother, Paul—was awkward. No one knew what to say about the race, so we chose to say nothing.

We visited for a while in the living room before my mom and dad went off to bed. Just before they did, my dad handed me a box filled with newspaper clippings from the Games. They were all from the *St. Catharines Standard* and the *Globe and Mail*. It was late, but my internal clock was so messed up I didn't feel much like sleeping. After Paul went to bed, I sat down in the living room with our dog. Tiger was a beagle-Brittany spaniel cross we'd named after the Hamilton Tiger Cats, a Canadian Football League team that had their training camps at Ridley during late summer. As a pup, Tiger had shown up on the playing fields during practice one day and one of the team managers brought him into our backyard thinking he belonged to us. I convinced my parents that we should at least take care of him until his owners showed up. They never did, and Tiger would end up spending the next 13 years with us.

With Tiger by my side, I started going through the box of newspaper clippings. Most were about Johnson's win and his eventual fall from grace. When I came across the front page of the *Globe and Mail* from the day of our final, there we were, in full colour, slumped over our oars at the finish of our race with the headline "Canadians Bomb Out in Seoul."

Seeing that photo took me right back to that moment. I could hear the sounds of the West Germans celebrating. Reading that headline brought the pain. I suddenly felt like someone was smashing a two-by-four across my chest.

Jim Proudfoot, who had written the article, went on about how we had not produced what was expected of us and that Rowing Canada had a lot to answer for given that Canada had won gold in Los Angeles in 1984. He wanted to know who was to blame and who was going to take the fall? The disappointment, I realized, wasn't just private. It was public too. I was pissed. This was my race to answer for, and that was a personal process that I would do on my time. How dare this man make this thing public? How dare he talk about us like that? I felt angry, but for the first time since the race I felt another emotion, one that I would struggle with for years to come—shame.

2

LIFE GOES ON

Before I left for Seoul, I had secured a job as a rowing coach at Melbourne Grammar School, a boys' school in Australia. I was thrilled. The Canadian and Australian teams had always gotten along well at international regattas. The Aussies were a wild and fun bunch with no pretensions—just down-to-earth good guys. During my time in Melbourne I expected to train, but not full time. I needed a break—mentally more than anything. Along with maintaining my fitness, I figured I would work and earn some money so I could travel and have some fun before I came home. After that, I would resume my full-time training and go after Olympic gold in Barcelona—the host country for 1992. By winning that gold I would redeem myself with revenge and retribution. I would right the wrong of 1988. I would set the record straight.

I spent the next few weeks arranging my travel, packing, seeing friends and family, and learning how to scull (two oars, one in each hand), whereas previously I had only swept (one large oar, pulled with both hands). I was keeping busy, but there wasn't an hour of the day when I didn't think of the race in Seoul. It was on everyone else's minds too. When I met up with friends or family they all had the same question, "What happened?" Anytime I was introduced at a gathering it was, "This is Jason. He just got back from competing in the Olympics." And the next question would be, "Oh yeah? How'd you do?"

"Not so great," was my standard line.

"Oh well, at least you got to go."

Go? GO? You don't get it, do you? Going wasn't the point. I didn't train for all of those years and give up all that I did just to go. I went there to win. Rowing is not about going—it's not about a trip and a tracksuit—it's about winning gold medals. And, we didn't. That means we failed. And, right now, I'm having a really hard time swallowing that. Okay? So don't try to sugar-coat a shitty situation with "At least you got to go."

That was what I wanted to say. Instead, I would smile and say, "Yeah, I suppose."

What drove me crazy about the "what happened?" question was that I didn't have an answer. I didn't know what had happened. I only knew what hadn't happened: we didn't race to our potential. We didn't win. We lost. Period. The more I thought about it, the more it ate away at me. The result was that my confidence was starting to waver. When I went downtown or to the local shopping mall to run errands, I felt as though everyone had read the article and seen the picture and knew who I was, what I had done—or hadn't done. I felt as though everyone was staring at me, talking about me. Naturally, I started keeping my head down.

My subconscious life was suffering too. At least two or three times a week I would dream about the race. The dreams were different every time, but the result was always the same: we lost. I would always wake up afterwards and lie awake for a long while going over "what ifs." What if we had chosen to false start? What if I had yelled something and ignited the boat the way Kevin had two days earlier? Every day, going to Australia was becoming more of an escape for me; I couldn't wait to go. Just to get away. No more awkward introductions. No more embarrassing explanations. No more shame.

After a series of milk run flights from hell, I finally landed in Melbourne. I was picked up at the airport by a parent of one of the school's students. We drove along beautiful highways lined with palm trees and other tropical vegetation. It was like nothing I had ever seen before. And it was hot. I suddenly felt at ease about my decision. This trip and job was going to be just what I needed—time to escape the constant reminder of the Olympics.

We drove to the Yarra River, which is smack in the middle of the city, and pulled up to series of boathouses, each one filled to the rafters with rowing shells. High schools, universities and national team athletes all trained there. I was shown to the coaches' office, where four guys were sitting around a table enjoying an afternoon glass of wine. We shook hands and went through formal introductions. Then John Roxborough, who had arranged for me to coach there, asked, "So, what happened to you lot in that Olympic final?"

I started my job almost as soon as I arrived. John was the head of rowing and the senior boys' (rowers under 19) coach, and I worked for him. He was certainly from the old school of coaching—he liked to "row the piss out of them," as he would say. Neil was also about work and a lot of it, but it had to be good-quality training. He always told us where the finish line was, how many pieces we'd be doing, and for how long. John, on the other hand, would tell his boys to pull as hard as they could until he told them to stop. I didn't agree with this approach. As far as I was concerned, rowing full pressure forever was impossible.

Once in a while I would fill in for one of the junior boys' coaches. Those were fun days for me—in some ways a welcome break from the intensity of coaching the senior crew. These young boys just loved rowing—period. It didn't matter what kind of boat they were in or where they were sitting, as far as they were concerned they were rowing and that was exciting enough. Watching them reminded me of how I used to see rowing as fun. Each time I had a new group of novice rowers, I explained that, although technique was important, pulling hard was more important. I told them that every stroke was a competition: a chance to see who liked to pull harder—you or the other guys.

I would set up a game, one side against the other—port against starboard. For 10 strokes they would pull as hard as they could and see who could turn the boat. Two at time, they would compete against one another, and we would keep track of which side had won. Then I would get them to do it again, encouraging the rowers who had been *turned* to find a way to generate more force. They loved it.

I was a different coach with the top crews. I shared all of the head games I used before a race with these teenage athletes. I coached what I knew, and what I knew was war. Because I was such an angry competitor, it was no surprise that I was an angry coach. I instilled in these young boys everything that I knew as an athlete: that you hate your competition and that winning a race was about killing your competition. What began as a small notion of how to be accepted and deemed worthy by my own high school rowing peers grew into my default modus operandi. Unknowingly my rowing— and coaching—demons were multiplying inside of me. Demons that would soon knock me on my ass.

The rowing nightmares became more frequent. Sometimes I was racing; other times just training. Frequently, guys from my high school crews were in the boat. I would awake from these dreams in a foul mood that would stay with me for the rest of the day. Our loss in Seoul and my reaction to it were turning me into a bitter young man. Then I discovered I hadn't cornered the entire market for being pissed off about the result of that race.

During my early days in Australia, I had met with a number of the national sculling team and one of them had lent me his boat.

One day, after a row, a group of us were standing around shooting the breeze, and the men's eight final in Seoul came up. The Australian men's eight had come fifth, just half a second ahead of us, but where my anger and frustration was directed inward, theirs was directed outward at the West Germans. The broken equipment thing was the source of a lot of discussion, and many guys thought the West Germans had used the broken equipment as a scam to cause a distraction and throw the other countries off their games.

Our crew had never even talked about the race, let alone whether or not the West German equipment failure might have been a ploy that would ultimately assist them in claiming Olympic gold. I had never even really thought about it myself. I'd just assumed their claim was legitimate and that they had in fact broken something and we, their competition, had allowed them the chance to fix it so that we could all race fairly. Winning by cheating is an empty victory void of satisfaction. I listened to the Aussies' theories but never really bought into them. I did notice one thing: unlike me, it seemed that even though they were pissed off about the outcome and their performance, they had generally gotten on with things.

The Australian National High School Championships were in a few weeks and we had a lot of work to do. Our senior crew was made up of some very big rowers, most of them six feet or taller. They were strong and committed to going fast, but they had not really hit their stride all season. John was at his wits' end trying to figure out what was wrong. His usual remedy was to continue to row the piss out of them some more. That wouldn't have been my choice, but it wasn't my crew. Many times I felt like a spectator in the coach boat. John had his opinions and he didn't want to know mine. I couldn't blame him, though. I understood the mindset of trying to figure out the challenges of coaching on your own.

The national championships came and went with the Melbourne Grammar senior boat not even making the final. It was a disappointing season for everyone involved, myself included. After the regatta, one of the parents hosted a party to close off the season. Following some kind words of appreciation, the crew presented me with an Australian Akubra hat. Given that I hadn't done my job—helped them win—I felt funny accepting their generous gift. Even though I'd had a limited impact on their season, I still felt the familiar kick to the groin of losing.

After a few more weeks of work, then many thanks and goodbyes, I boarded a bus heading north—I was on my way home. I had successfully applied for the position of junior (rowers under 16) coach at Shawnigan Lake School on Vancouver Island. The job was perfect. It would allow me to coach and to train on an enormous freshwater lake where I would begin my comeback. But first, I was going to spend a month touring the east coast of Australia and spending all of my hard-earned money.

My first stop was Sydney where I met up with Dale Petersen, the coxie of the Aussie men's eight. On my first night we went out for dinner, and Dale showed me some of the sights. There was little talk of the final in Seoul other than a few choice words from Dale about the West Germans. The next morning, I was off to Surfers Paradise to meet up with the stroke of the Aussie eight, Stephen Evans. The rest of my trip was about as magical as one could imagine. The places I went, the things I saw and the people I met were all wonderful.

A young English woman named Katy became my travelling companion for the better part of three weeks. We went sailing, snorkelling, surfing, hiking—you name it, we did it. I travelled with my Canadian team bags from our trip to Seoul, so it was hard not to notice where I had been. When she asked the inevitable question, I gave her my standard answer—"Not so great"—and that was it. She wasn't too impressed that I had been to the Olympics, and she didn't seem to care that I had lost. The conversation ended there, never to be raised again. I don't believe it was because she didn't want to hurt my feelings; she just wasn't all that interested. She was just what I needed at the time—someone who just enjoyed being. I was constantly in awe of Katy's ability to be so content in the moment, for no reason other than she was alive and there to experience whatever it was we were experiencing. I never felt judged around her and that was a welcome respite from the judgment that I constantly dished out on myself. In addition, Katy made me realize for the first time that not everyone's life revolved around sport.

I arrived back in St. Catharines in July 1989. A lot had changed while I was away. My parents had moved, and our dog, Tiger, was gone. He had started to lose his faculties. The decision to put Tiger down was a hard one for my dad. I also found out that many other guys from the national team had chosen to take the year off from rowing. A few had stayed on and were training for the World Championships in Bled, Slovenia.

My pair partner, Darby Berkhout, was one of them. He had been in the men's straight four (a boat with four rowers and no coxie) in Seoul. They had finished out of the final but hadn't expected to be in the top six. Darby had met his own expectations and, as a result, the Olympics had been quite positive for him. Questions about the race in Seoul were less frequent than before I left, and Darby, like most people just wanted to know about my trip to Australia. It had been almost a year since our race and it appeared that everybody had forgotten about our performance or just wasn't interested anymore—everybody but me.

I spent the summer in St. Catharines and then arranged to drive out west with Tim Coy, a good friend and ex-coxie from our days at both Ridley and the University of Victoria (UVic). Like me, he was a staff brat raised at Ridley. His dad was a history teacher, as well as a football and hockey coach, who had taught and coached me when I was in Lower School.

To get to Vancouver Island, Tim and I decided to use a drive-away company to make the journey. We got dropped off just outside of Toronto at the dealer's lot, where we were given a Subaru XT, a small sports car that could go like stink but didn't have much luggage room. After some creative packing, we began our trek. We had seven days to make it to Vancouver. It was a trip I had made before and have many times since. It's one that I never grow tired of because it reminds me of how fortunate I am to live in one of the most beautiful countries in the world.

Besides being an excellent coxie, Tim was also an extremely funny guy. He had the uncanny ability of watching a movie once and remembering almost every line. Right from the start of our trip, Tim was an unending source of entertainment, rambling off scenes from some recent comedies. Not only could he recite the lines flawlessly, he could assume each character's voice. His unending jokes made for one hilarious trip; the miles passed quickly. Five days after leaving Toronto, with a short stopover in Calgary, we had reached the final leg of our journey.

The West Coast is probably the most beautiful place I have ever lived. There's something quite serene and magic about pulling away from the ferry terminal in Tsawwassen, just outside of Vancouver, the start of the trip to Swartz Bay on Vancouver Island. That night in late August 1989, I stood on the deck of the ferry and watched the sun set. The receding hues over the Gulf Islands made a mystical backdrop for the epic quest I saw before me. *These welcoming skies*, I thought, *will witness my comeback*. In that moment, I promised myself that, for the next three years, I would not compromise. I would train harder than ever before. I would find new limits everyday. I would show everyone what I was truly capable of. More importantly, I would show everyone that I was no loser.

To help me accomplish this goal, I had brought along a secret weapon. It was the photograph from the front page of the *Globe*, the one of our team slumped over our oars. My dad had purchased it for me. I wasn't sure why he had bothered. He knew me well enough to know I wouldn't want a picture of me losing my Olympic gold medal. I think he believed that a day would come where I would see the photo for more than it was to me now—a reminder of my shortcoming. That night onboard the ferry, I was indeed glad he had ordered the photograph because in that moment captured on film I found purpose—the source of a commanding new motivation.

In the coming months, before each of my rows and at night before bed, I would pull out that picture and go back to that moment. Back to the sounds, the sights and the physical pain. Back to the emotions that still owned me: frustration, humiliation, shame and rage. Most of all, it was this new level of rage that I felt toward my competitors. I believed back then that that enraged fury was going to bring me to a new level of preparation.

From the ferry dock, Tim grabbed a bus to Victoria while I caught one travelling north up Vancouver Island. My instructions were to get off in Mill Bay where someone from the school would meet me. No sooner had I taken my luggage off the bus than an old blue Toyota Land Cruiser pulled up. The passenger-side window rolled down revealing a man with big smile. It was Peter Yates. He had rowed as a lightweight at the University of British Columbia (UBC) during the late '70s and early '80s. When a lack of coaches at UBC threatened the program, Peter had jumped at the opportunity to try coaching. Now, along with teaching English, he was the head of rowing at Shawnigan, which had a decent reputation as a rowing school. Peter had done an amazing job building a program at a school that was obsessed with rugby. He was the head coach, the boat repairman, the administrator and the sport's main advocate. You name it and chances were Peter had had his hand in making sure it was run to the best of his ability.

Later that day, I found out that Shawnigan had hired another Olympian, Andrea Schreiner, to coach rowing also. Andrea had been one of the top Canadian women's scullers in the 1980s. She had a silver medal from the 1984 Olympics in Los Angeles and had competed at numerous World Championships and international regattas, winning dozens of medals throughout her career. We had been on the same team in 1986 but hadn't trained in the same city, so we didn't know each other that well. I was thrilled to be working with someone of her knowledge and experience.

Within the first few days, she sat down with me and mapped out a weight-training regimen over a seven-week cycle. I hadn't thrown weights around for months, so before I could begin performing cleans and squats with any amount of weight, I had to get my tendons and muscles ready. Initially, I did three weeks of calisthenics that used my own body weight. As eager as I was to get started and surpass my strength prior to Seoul, I knew I had to be smart about it. In the past I had gotten myself into trouble by doing too much too soon and then having to take time off to rest. I knew Andrea would ensure that I properly tracked my progress and increased my workload appropriately. I knew she wouldn't let me get stupid about it.

My job as a rowing coach didn't start until the beginning of the winter term so I was asked to coach the junior girls' volleyball team— Grade 8s and 9s—for the fall term. I'd never coached volleyball (or teenaged girls) before, but with Andrea coaching the senior girls on the court beside me, I was able to learn what I needed to know. Over the first few weeks, I picked up a number of useful coaching tips and drills. As the season progressed, however, I felt comfortable enough to do things on my own. The day before our first match against a local school, I asked Andrea what Shawnigan's policy was on competition—was it win at all costs or focus on participation?

"It would be a good thing if you won some games. But remember, Jase. This isn't the Olympics. This is junior girls' volleyball."

Unfortunately, I didn't hear the part about it not being the Olympics—all I heard was "win a few games."

My strategy was to establish a first line and a second line. The first line played for the majority of the matches while the second line stood behind the bench, waiting and hoping for the chance to play. Ultimately, they never did see much action—until one fateful day.

We were playing an afternoon game against a local school in Duncan. We had won the first game and were well on our way to winning the second when one of the girls standing behind the bench tapped me on my shoulder.

"Hold on a sec," I said.

Then, another tap. "Mr. Dorland?"

"Wait for a whistle," I snapped back.

Finally, a third tap. "Mr. Dorland!"

I spun around quickly to see what was so important. "What, Natalie? What do you want?"

I glared at her, obviously pissed off that she had interrupted my concentration on the game.

"When do we get to play?" she asked quietly, her eyes tearing up and her voice shaking with fear.

Wham!

It hit me right in the gut. *Jase, look at this kid—she's in tears because of you. You and your gotta-win-every-game approach. Good job, buddy. Now there's one to be proud of—you've just made a 13-year-old cry.*

"Now. Right now," I responded. "You get to play right now."

I stood up and immediately called for a substitution. One by one, I subbed each of the second line on and did so until the end of the match.

We not only won that match, we went on to become one of the top junior teams on Vancouver Island. More importantly, we became a team obsessed with fun. Practices were still hard, but the focus was on having fun, and everyone saw an equal amount of court time. As a result, everyone's skills improved drastically; the girls on the second line improved to the same level as the first line and, in the process, had a blast. To my amazement we discovered that if we became too intent on winning a game, we would tighten up and play poorly. When we settled down and focused on having fun, we actually won more games. It was a good lesson for me, but one that was short-lived and only worked on the volleyball court. When the winter term arrived, and the rowing season began, the fun and laughter went out the window, and the war resumed.

I was assigned to the Colt boys—who were the same age as the girls I had just coached in volleyball—plus the Grade 10s. We began the season with plenty of land training, including running and calisthenics. It was an old habit I'd found hard to let go of. I was not used to the notion that you rowed yourself into shape. At Ridley, by the time we got on the water in March, we were extremely fit and ready to start training right from the first day. At Shawnigan, even though the guys had played rugby during the first term, they weren't in rowing shape.

Brentwood College School, the local rival, was a few miles down the road. Tony Carr was the head coach. He had built one of the most successful high school rowing programs in the world. The school's location was part of the reason. The waves of the Pacific Ocean lapped up onto the school's campus in Mill Bay. The postcard scenery was ideal for someone who had Tony's vision. Although Shawnigan was idyllically located as well, the focus on rowing had never existed the way it had at Brentwood. Instead, Shawnigan had always hung its hat on its successful rugby program.

I liked the fact that rowing at Shawnigan was in many ways a poor cousin to rugby. I preferred the notion of operating under the radar without much hype or fanfare. Neil had always taught us to do our talking with our oars, not with our mouths, so I was quite content to work at a school where most people didn't really notice what I was doing. This was probably a good thing given that nothing had changed with my coaching philosophy since Australia. The same war tactic that I had used as the main source of inspiration for my rowers there worked equally as well on these young Canadian boys. In fact, if anything, I had ramped it up a little with my new crew.

As for my own training, things were progressing about as well as I could have hoped. In less than two months, I was lifting as much or more weight than I had been before I'd left for Seoul. I was making headway with my technique, and my fitness was returning as my weekly time trials improved.

The lake was approximately seven and a half kilometres long, so I could row for a long time without having to turn around. When I was a teen training on Martindale Pond in Port Dalhousie near St. Catharines, we had to stop and turn every 2,000 metres—the length of a rowing race. At Shawnigan, in a single (a one-person rowing shell), you could row for 40 minutes in one direction. Not only that, but the lake hardly saw any motorboat traffic after September, so I didn't have to contend with pleasure boats or their wakes—a sore point for most rowers.

I had landed in training heaven: room and board, a small paycheque every month, a decent weight room and a world-class coach to help me out on a regular basis. Given how much I could eat when I was training, having my meals included was a bonus. Although the food was institutional, it was as good as or better than most school food I had ever eaten, and the young chef had dreams of opening his own restaurant, so he routinely tried out new dishes on me. In other words, life was good.

Emotionally, I considered myself fine. My secret weapon, as I continued to refer to my new motivation, was working like a charm.

I regularly visited Seoul by looking at the photograph, and that added the intended purpose and fire to each workout; however, my nightmares continued, constantly reminding me that the bitterness surrounding that race was still unresolved. What had changed was that my internal critic was no longer using the plural tense when discussing the loss in Seoul—what had "we" done to lose the race. Instead, he was now using the singular—what had "I" done to lose the race. My internal critic had convinced me that perhaps, maybe, I was to blame. After all, I was the last one to make the boat. I was the lightest guy. I was one of the youngest and most inexperienced.

The more I choked down the theory that I had lost the race for the team, the harder I wanted to train. I wanted to prove that it wasn't my fault, that I hadn't caused us to lose. Because simply talking about the race was out of my comfort zone, no matter how much I felt I could trust someone, confessing my guilt was not going to happen. Imagine the phone call, "Hey, Neil, guess what? I finally figured out why we lost—it was me!" The shame associated with that admission made it out of the question.

One day, almost a year to the day of the Seoul race, Jens Gotthardt, a sports enthusiast and science teacher at Shawnigan, approached me. He wanted me to talk to his class about my Olympic experience. I tried to discourage the idea. I told him that I really wasn't that comfortable speaking in front of a large group. I added, "Besides, we lost. Why would they want to hear about that?"

He looked at me strangely. "Don't be stupid, there's a lot to share with them. Tell them what it was like to represent your country at an Olympic Games. Tell them anything—they'll love it."

Love it? Love what? Love that we lost? Love that I was a loser? What the hell was he talking about? What was I going to say? It was great? It was the best experience of my life?

The students were all smiles and excitement when they filed into the classroom. Although I had been at the school for a while,

I didn't know many of them. I was only involved with students I either coached or knew through Groves' House, the boarding house with which I was affiliated. I smiled and introduced myself.

"Mr. Gotthardt asked me to come in here and talk about my Olympic experience—I think that's what he referred to it as. Trouble is, I had a bunch of experiences and I'm not sure which one you want to hear about."

"Tell us about your race? How did it go?"

I waited, and then took a deep breath and began. I told them that we had gone to Seoul to do one thing—to win. I went over the details of our first two races. I explained how, if we could have put the first part of our heat and the last part of our repechage together, we would have had a good shot at winning. Then, I talked about the final and about the delay because of the West German team's broken equipment. I told them we were tied for first at the 500-metre mark despite our slow start and then I told them how it all slipped away. Finally, I told them what losing felt like.

"When people watch the Olympics on TV, or any sports competition for that matter, all they care about is who wins. Me too—I'm the same way. That's all I care about—who won? And when we turn off the television, it's over, right? I mean, we stop thinking about it. We never wonder how the losers are feeling."

By that point I was staring blankly at the back of the room; the students could've gotten up and walked out and I wouldn't have noticed. I was that lost in the moment.

"When we crossed the finish line, and I realized we had lost, I wanted the boat to fill up with water and sink. I wanted to drown." I paused as my throat locked up—I couldn't speak. My quivering chin brought me back into the room and once again I noticed the students in front of me. The horrified looks on their faces all said the same thing, "Holy shit, he's going to cry."

I could sense that a train wreck was fast approaching. I was frozen with fear. Not a word would come out and I could feel tears coming on. For the first time since our final, I was explaining to someone else how losing that gold medal had felt, and it struck me that this was a bad idea. They didn't need to hear this. Hell, I didn't need to hear this—I was done talking. Trying desperately to regain some composure, I spun around and hit the play button on the video machine. "Here—you can see for yourself."

My brother Paul had recorded our final on VHS and had given me the tape when I got home. I hadn't seen all of it. It was unbearable for me to watch beyond the 500-metre mark, at which point the Brits and everyone else started to move away and leave us to struggle through the remainder of the race. As I stood there listening and watching, I began to shake. After a few moments, I reached out and managed to hit the eject button despite my trembling hands.

"Here, watch this one instead. This is how you win an Olympic gold medal." I shoved in another video and hit PLAY.

It was a quintessential and beautiful race—one that I never got tired of watching—the 1984 Los Angeles Olympics men's eight race where Canada won the gold. I remember being in our living room with some of the guys that I was rowing with that summer. We were young and obsessed with rowing. There had been a lot of hype leading up to this race, as the Canadians had defeated the American crew several times in Europe earlier that summer. Neil's crew had also beaten the East Germans and the Russians at those same regattas but they weren't in Los Angeles because of the boycott, so the race was touted as a rematch between the United States and Canada.

As any good rematch would have it, the two crews were side by side in the final. The Canadians took an early lead. We knew most of the guys in Neil's boat—we revered them. As far as we were concerned, there was no way they could lose. At the 1,000-metre mark, the Canadians had increased their lead to almost three-quarters of a boat length. Just after the halfway point, the Canadians made another move, increasing their lead to a boat length, which is equivalent to about three seconds on the rest of the field. Although the United States would mount a courageous charge, they not only ran out of space, they also ran out of steam, and the Canadians held on to win the gold medal, setting an Olympic record time of 5 minutes and 41 seconds. They had won—in classic Neil Campbell style—by getting out ahead and staying there. It was quite possibly, and remains to this day, one of the most exciting races in rowing history. When the tape was over, I shut off the machine and turned to face a class full of smiling students. They too had been captured by the race and impressed with the efforts of the Canadian crew.

"What happened to those guys? Were any of them in your boat?"

"Yup. Three of the rowers and the coxie."

"So what happened?" one boy asked. "Why didn't you guys win again?"

With that, a girl sitting in the front row turned and gave the boy a look that must have said, "Shut up!"

Because he looked at her and replied quietly, "What?"

She then turned to me and asked, "What was it like living in the athletes' village?"

Saved!

"Well, it was fun," I said. "We met people from all over the world. I realized, as corny as it may sound, that we're really not all that different from one another. For instance, every night athletes from different countries would go out on their balconies and make paper airplanes and launch them into the air to see whose could fly the farthest. People would cheer and clap. On one hand, it was quite childish, but on the other, for a few moments each night we were just young people from different cultures who didn't speak a common language but were united by something as simple as a paper airplane. That had allowed each of us to forget about the worries and pressures of being there."

I also told them about the water balloons that we dropped on anyone and everyone who stood too close to our building.

"A few days after our race, just before we were heading home, someone noticed our team manager, Jimmy Joy, standing right below our balcony, which was six storeys up. We sprang into action, found the biggest garbage bin we could, filled it with as much water as we could lift—which was a lot—then dragged it over to the edge of the balcony. We watched as the mass of tumbling water fell toward its target. Bull's eye!

Regardless of why we did it and how stupid it was, the students seemed to get a kick out of it. Similar stories filled the remaining time in that fateful class. When it was over and the students had left, I was alone waiting for the videos to rewind. Listening to the whirring VCR, it bothered me that sharing my Olympic experience was something I felt shameful about. It occurred to me that going to the Olympics should be a highlight of a person's life, not a dark secret. Those students should have left believing the Olympics can be any person's dream and a moment in their life that they will be proud of forever. Instead, I had painted a depressing and regrettable experience. At the end of the day, I buried all the emotions that had surfaced that afternoon and went on with my quest for my gold medal and for revenge.

3 ■▶———

A SECOND CHANCE

Marius Felix was a big man. In his prime, he stood 6'7" and weighed in at 220 pounds. He had come out of Tony Carr's program at Brentwood College during the mid-1970s and then travelled south to the University of Washington where he rowed for another rowing legend, Dick Erickson. While there, Marius stroked one of the most famous college crews ever. In 1980, Marius had made the Canadian Olympic men's eight for the Moscow Olympics. Unfortunately, many countries, including Canada, boycotted the Games over the Soviet invasion of Afghanistan. Where I was struggling with my performance in Seoul, Marius hadn't even been given the chance to perform. Marius's size made him a natural in any number of sports, so after the disappointment of the boycott he hung up his oar for good and started playing rugby. Now he taught at Shawnigan and coached the rugby team. Sharing a common love of competitive sport, he would often invite me over for some good chats over a bowl of his famous curried rice.

One evening, midway through bowl number three, Marius asked how my training was going. I said I was having trouble with the winter blahs. Without any hesitation, he offered to come down to the weight room and work out with me a few times a week. He was welcome company indeed, and added inspiration. His size was reminiscent of the West Germans, which reminded me how much harder I had to train to win back my gold medal.

It worked—I was able to regain my stride, and my training continued as well as I could have hoped. By late January of 1990, my on-water workouts were also the best they had been in four months. The head games I was playing spurred me on to faster and faster times. Sure, I was still using the same retribution card as my main source of inspiration, but now I had a new weapon to add to my arsenal. When I was in the midst of a piece and my mind started to complain about the pain, I would force myself to pull harder on the next stroke—then harder again the next stroke after that. I was trying to teach myself not to let up by punishing my body for even entertaining the notion. I figured that if I made myself hurt more, then I wouldn't think about letting up in the first place.

What I discovered was that as I continued to ignore my mind's requests to stop and forced myself beyond the pain, I would enter a state, both physical and mental, that I can only describe as complete numbness. It took a bit of doing to get there, and the process hurt like hell, but once I arrived, it was powerful—I loved it. To have that much control over my body was euphoric. I looked forward to the workouts so I could experience the high of going that hard, that fast and that far. It was a huge boost to my confidence. I was proving to myself that, even at this stage in my career, new limits were possible with every day and every workout.

The problem was that I began to take some of my internal pain and turmoil out on the young boys I was coaching. They were improving steadily—getting fitter and faster—but it was all about getting ready to do battle with the competition when regatta season started. Sometimes, I would get so mad when things didn't go well that I didn't recognize myself. What I said and how I said it were beyond any level of anger and aggression that most parents would have considered normal or acceptable—I was out of control.

After the disappointing performances of many of the crews in Seoul, Rowing Canada had decided to go offshore and find someone to put the national team program back together, someone who had taken crews to the front of the world stage and wasn't afraid to make radical changes. They chose Britain's Mike Spracklen for his many years of international coaching experience. His most famous rower was Steven Redgrave, who had won numerous World Championship and Olympic gold medals. Redgrave was an enormous man who made an oar look small in his hands. Spracklen, on the other hand, didn't look the part; he was tiny, and when he spoke, which wasn't often, it was softly.

Word came that Spracklen would be holding a weeklong rowing camp in March 1990 at Elk Lake, just outside Victoria on the Island. Mike was keen to start the long process of formulating an Olympic team for Barcelona in 1992. Darby Berkhout was flying out from Ontario for the camp and would be joining me on Tim Coy's basement floor for the week.

After giving my crews' workouts to the other junior boys' coach, I was ready to go. This was it—my return to the arena of competitive rowing. Granted, not something you would hear about on the evening news, but in my little world, it was about as important as things got. I defined myself by my success in rowing, and this was my first opportunity to let others know that I was back—and in a big way.

The buzz about Mike and what he might bring to the program brought out lots of athletes. All of the rowers and coaches in attendance crammed into one of the meeting rooms at Elk Lake where the national team trained. As expected, Spracklen was soft spoken and direct with his message. He listed the technical changes he wanted to implement and explained his ideas concerning the amount of workload an athlete could handle during peak training. He used a great analogy—our bodies respond to training like the skin on our hands responds to the friction of pulling on an oar when we row. When you rub hard enough against the skin, the body responds by creating a blister. Then you continue to rub and stress the skin, and the blister eventually heals, hardens and turns into a callus. As you stress the area further, the callus gets tougher to accommodate the added friction. Our entire bodies were the same—if we stress our muscles they respond by getting stronger to handle the work should it happen again. When it does, the body reacts again, continually building stronger muscles the more frequently and harder you train.

I loved it; however, when I saw the prescribed training sessions for the week, I was shocked at the amount of mileage that he had planned. It was a lot, but like most of the others in the room, I was up for the challenge.

After the meeting we made our way down to the front of the boathouse to receive our boating orders. I was pleased to see that the rest of the guys from Seoul had decided to return. There were also some new faces—younger rowers who were now taking their first shot at the national team.

For the first row, I was in a single. That was fine with me; I wanted to show everyone, especially Spracklen, that I had been training hard at Shawnigan and that I had come here to do business. We were given a flow pattern to adhere to and prescribed a certain number of kilometres to cover, with a designated rate and pressure. As others shoved off, I was stuck on the dock struggling with my foot stretchers (adjustable footplates which allow you to change your position relative to the slide and the oarlock) and tracks.

Racing shells are designed to accommodate all different types of bodies—long legs and short bodies or short bodies and long legs. Foot stretchers and tracks are supposed to be adjustable but there I was, 15 minutes past the start time, stuck on the dock trying to make adjustments that would enable me not only to have a more comfortable row, but also a better one—a faster one. As I pushed, pulled and eventually bashed the parts that wouldn't move, I grew more and more frustrated and was soon cursing out loud. Eventually I was able to move my stretchers enough to get into the boat and row away from the dock. I had to catch up to the rest of the group, which was now well into the workout. Then, because of the mechanical problems I was having with my boat, I couldn't apply full pressure. Not being able to join in with the workout, I rowed through the channel and tried to put together some sort of a training session on my own.

Spracklen came alongside to see what the matter was. In a quiet and polite manner, Mike asked, "Exactly what is the problem, Jason?"

"I can't get this fuckin' boat to work," I yelled at him. "I don't know—these stupid tracks won't move. They're jammed and I can't use full pressure."

"Well there's no point getting upset about it," he said. "Let's have a look." Mike pulled his boat in close to mine to inspect the problem. Even with his tools, he was unable to move the tracks. "They appear to be jammed," he confirmed. "Just head in and we'll have them fixed for the next row."

I turned my boat toward the docks and began to row in. I was furious. My one chance to make a good first impression with the one guy who could help me win back my gold medal—my self-respect—and what did I do? I screamed and cursed at him. I had made a first impression on Mike all right; I had shown him that I was a spoiled little brat with a bad temper. *Good one, Jase!*

With my boat fixed, it was soon time for our next row—steady-state pressure (pressure that resembled going for a long run—firm, but not full-out) with a focus on drills. We were left on our own, so I was able to calm down. My row this time was decent, and I felt encouraged coming off the water. After lunch, the workout involved short bursts of speed at a high rate mixed in with long, powerful strokes at a lower rate. It would be a great test to see where my speed was relative to the others.

After what I felt was a good warm-up, we met at one end of the lake and began the first piece. During my warm-up, I went through my usual routine of building intense hatred and anger toward my competitors—*Don't just win, Jase, kill them!*—but this time my competitors were rowing beside me and not in my head as they had for the past six months at Shawnigan. Back at Shawnigan I was able to imagine my competitors racing alongside, but ultimately I could maintain my focus on each stroke. Now, with an actual boat—someone to race—a few feet to my left and right, I was finding it too distracting. The more I worried about winning each piece and destroying my competition, the worse I rowed and the slower I went. More rage did not equal more speed—anything but.

It was a horrible row, undoubtedly the worst since September. I was more than capable of going as fast as or faster than anyone out there, but I just couldn't do it. *What's wrong? You're getting beat by losers. Go harder!*

The more that internal dialogue escalated, the worse it got, until I had spiralled so far down, there was no way I was going to turn the workout around. I got thoroughly beaten by the other rowers. As I rowed toward the dock, the workout over, it was clear that the speed I had discovered in the past month at school—the new physical and mental limits—had eluded me.

Simply put, while the other rowers had focused on the task at hand—rowing properly and going fast—I had worried about the outcome and was unable to reach the limits of my ability. My psychological games had backfired. What good was my secret weapon if it didn't help me win? Clearly my anger-infused approach to competition had boiled over and made a mess of the day.

That night, there was a dinner for everyone at Mike Spracklen's house. I hadn't seen most of the guys in over a year, so we spent the better part of the night catching up. There was no talk of Seoul, or even much about the 1989 World Championships, in which the Canadians had, once again, underperformed. Instead, everyone talked about the future and what Spracklen would do for the national team. Although I had a restless night's sleep, I was up and ready the next day for the new boating lineups. I would be rowing in a double scull with Brian Sanderson, a strong, stocky rower from Ontario. Brian was a member of the coxed four that finished fifth at the Worlds in 1987. In Seoul, his crew had hoped to build on that performance and win a medal, but they failed to make the final. Like many others, he had taken the year off and was now back to see what the future might hold.

Brian and I began the session with a decent warm-up. As we lined up and prepared to face off with the others, I was anxious to better my previous day's results. The horn sounded to signal the start of the first piece and, as I had done the day before, I immediately shifted my focus from us to the other boats around us. Needless to say, my anger and frustration grew with each piece until our boat was practically dead in the water. We didn't win a single race.

That afternoon, the same pathetic story unfolded. In race after race, my internal psychological warfare garnered the same results—a slow-moving boat with me in it. At the end of day two, I was thoroughly spent from trying so desperately to prove to the coaches, other rowers and myself that I was back and ready, that, at the end of six rows, I had impressed no one.

At 3:00 AM, I woke up feeling nauseated, aching, shivering, and soaking wet with sweat. I got up and made my way to the bathroom where I threw up. I had the flu. My rowing camp was over. There would be no third day of trying to win races. Later that day, I packed up my stuff and drove back to Shawnigan—defeated. At the time, I felt there was nothing positive that I could take away from the camp. I had been beaten thoroughly during the two days that I had managed to show up, and there were no excuses, no clear reasons that I could identify to cut myself some slack. Simply put, I had nothing to show for all of my efforts since September—my training had been for naught. I wasn't any closer to achieving revenge and, with it, regaining my self-respect.

My inability to race effectively at the camp played constantly in my head. Neil had always told us, "If you can't do it in practice, you can't do it on race day." But I could do it in practice—every day. When I was on my own at Shawnigan, I clocked times that would have, undoubtedly, won some races at the camp.

I decided that I would relax more during my workouts and resist the urge to get riled up. I needed to motivate myself without losing control. If I monitored my anger on the water, I could prepare for the next camp and seek redemption for my dismal performance. It worked, but only for a month. Suddenly, the training blahs that had struck me after Christmas returned with vengeance. The moment I awoke each morning, the great debate began:

No, don't get up. You're tired. Don't worry about it, just roll over and go back to sleep—you deserve it. You've been working hard.

Get out of bed, ya wimp! If you really wanted your medal back, we wouldn't be having this discussion. If you roll over, you don't deserve to go Barcelona. Because you know for sure the Germans, the Yanks, the Russians will all be training today. Get up, you loser!

It would go on and on like that, each voice having its turn until I finally crawled out of bed and put on my training clothes. Even though the get-up-and-row side always won, the effort it took to get down to the dock and out on the water was monumental. On my way to the lake, I tried to avoid people because I was so miserable. Once the workout was over, and I was rowing into the dock, I sometimes stopped to take in the scenery and appreciate just how fortunate I was to be training at Shawnigan, but those moments were soon overtaken with thoughts of the next training session.

Training for Seoul had never been like this. Sure, I'd had days where I was tired, but I'd loved the training and thrived on the challenge of each workout. It gave my life purpose and filled me with confidence and a sense of accomplishment every day. It was a time in my life when I'd felt a part of something and that each day had a reason: getting bigger, stronger, faster and one step closer to my dream—my Olympic gold medal.

This time, my experience was so different. I hated what my life had become: nothing more than a mindless routine of training, worrying about training and hating everything to do with training. Even my mind games had eased up. I was so tired of cranking myself up for each session by looking at my photo from Seoul that I just stopped doing it. The sessions had gone from trying to get faster to just trying to hang on and get through each one.

One day, while I was going down to the boathouse for my morning row, distracted by the usual argument with myself about possibly taking a day or two off from training, I almost got killed. About halfway across the road to the boathouse, I heard a car coming fast. I jumped back and managed to avoid being hit. I watched the car speed away, stunned, shocked at the thought of what might have happened and how serious it could have been if I hadn't jumped to safety. Then, while unlocking the door to the boathouse, I thought, *You know, if that car had hit me—I could've taken a few days off—maybe even a week. I could've stayed in bed, watched some movies, kicked back and relaxed.*

Jase, what the hell are you thinking? If that car had hit you, you could be dead. Shut up!

I shook my head to jar myself out of this conversation. I brought my oars down to the dock and went back to get my boat. It was a beautiful morning: the temperature was mild and the sun was beginning to break through the clouds. Most importantly, the water was flat—a perfect morning for a row. With my boat ready in the water, I reached across to secure the oarlock.

Okay, then if not dead then maybe just a slight tap—a scrape or a bruise—something that would take just a day or two to get over.

Immediately, I let go of the clasp and lay back on the dock. With my knees up and my arms stretched out on both sides, I lay there, my head resting on the hard wooden planks. I was petrified.

Jase, listen to what you're saying. If you don't want to row today— don't row. If you don't want to row tomorrow or ever again—you don't have to.

Who are you kidding, anyway? You can't keep this up for three more years—you'll go crazy. You'll push everyone in your life—your family, your friends, everyone who means so much to you—away in the process. If you don't want to row anymore—that's okay.

Besides, who are you really doing this for? Who is this all about? Your dad? Your family? Neil? Who? Why are you banging your head against the wall like this? This is messed up, buddy.

"Okay, fine—I hear you. I get the point." I answered aloud.

And then there was nothing. No pointed chatter—just the sound of the water lapping against the dock. The mood was like a couple that has said too much and realizes they are in the midst of breaking up. I was in the midst of breaking up—with my dream. For years it had been the one dream I had wanted to come true more than anything else in my life.

I lay still for what seemed like another hour before I even blinked. Then, all at once, I stood up, grabbed my oars and then my boat, and put them away. I was done. I wasn't rowing today or tomorrow or ever again—I had quit.

I walked back to the school and went straight to Peter Yates's house. I knocked on the door. He answered and asked me in.

Sensing something was up, Peter went to put the kettle on. Although he was my boss, he had become my friend as well—like a big brother keeping an eye on me from a distance. He had an uncanny ability to listen and truly absorb what was being shared and then, only when he had heard everything, offer up his take on the matter. He was wise beyond his years. Gentle and kind—I could talk with him about anything.

"I don't know if I can keep rowing."

Peter just stared, waiting for me to continue.

"I'm having a tough time motivating myself to train." I paused. "When I was training for Seoul, it was easy. Now, training for Barcelona—it's not so easy. It's harder."

After another long pause, Peter finally spoke. "Jason, why do you want to go to the Olympics again? Why do you want to—?"

Before he had finished I said, "To win a gold medal."

"That's it?" asked Peter.

"Yup. That's the only reason—why else would anyone want to go?"

"Let's say you go and you don't win. Let's say you come second? You lose again?"

"Then the last four years will have been a waste of time."

"Truly?" asked Peter.

"Yup."

"What then? Train for another four years?"

"I don't know."

"Well, if nothing else, Jason, I hope you leave here today convinced you should think about that." Peter smiled.

We talked for a while longer, mainly about life after rowing and what that could look like. Peter, ever mindful of how I must have been feeling, was painting that picture with all sorts of great possibilities. I wasn't so sure. I didn't know anything other than a life that was about rowing and only rowing.

I went back to my room and spent the rest of the day reflecting on my decision. Before it got too late back east in Ontario, I had some people to phone. The first was Darby—having been my pair partner and good friend, the least I could do was call him and let him know. I simply told him straight up that I was going to retire. He understood completely. He too was questioning whether he should keep going. He had other aspirations that involved finishing school and getting on with his business. Darby was such a hard worker, it didn't really matter what he did, he would find success.

My next call was a given—Neil. I was nervous. No, I was scared. As a teenager I used to phone Neil every evening after dinner and talk about the day's workout and what we had to do to get faster. Even then I got nervous dialling his phone number. Now, it wasn't just about phoning him—I was over that. This time it was about *why* I was calling him. I was about to tell the one person who had taught me, above all else, to "never, ever quit," that I was doing just that—quitting.

Neil wasn't much for small talk. "What's wrong, Jase?

"I don't think I can keep rowing, Neil."

There was a long pause. My heart was pounding. *Please tell me you understand. Please say it's okay to quit, just this one time. Please, Neil. Please.* I needed him to acknowledge that there was no other choice.

"You had enough?"

"I've had enough, Neil."

"Well then, to hell with it—go out and have some fun. You've been doin' this a long time, Jase."

I exhaled. I'm sure Neil could hear the relief in my voice. We talked a bit more. He shared some old stories that were guaranteed to make me laugh. I could feel his warm hand gently squeezing the back of my neck as he tried to cheer me up. I needed it more than he knew.

I hung up the phone feeling tremendously relieved and exhausted. I had needed to know that the man who had been more than just a coach to me all these years understood why I was quitting, and it appeared that he did. I walked over to my bed, sat down and began to reflect on all my years as a rower. It had been a great ride, and I wouldn't have traded it for anything. I had travelled to faraway places, met the most amazing people and competed against the best in the world. The individuals I'd rowed with were my closest friends and I loved them dearly. Rowing had defined me and in doing so had been good to me, and now I was going to say goodbye to it forever—we were officially done.

Held by the warm darkness of my small room, the sound of the old radiator thumping in the background, I started to cry—a little at first, then a lot. I curled up on my bed as all of the emotions from the past year washed over me. I began to shake and sob uncontrollably. Everything I had buried deep inside me so that I could stay motivated found a crack and was escaping to the surface as quickly as it could. I had never in my life cried like this before. If these were healing tears, they were coming fast and furious. They kept coming until I fell asleep.

The next morning I awoke from a deep restful sleep and realized that for the first time in many years I didn't have to get up and train—I was free to do whatever I wanted. So logically, I jumped out of bed, put my running stuff on and went for a very long run on the wooded trails around Shawnigan, not because it was on the training regimen for the day, but because it felt like the weight of the world had been lifted from my shoulders and I had so much energy that I had to do something. I knew in that moment that I had made the right decision. I felt truly alive for the first time in a long time.

As one hour turned into another, the trails kept getting easier. Charging through those evergreens, I decided that with my rowing finished I would need a new goal—something to chase, something to try to win. My coaching was the obvious choice. I would now put all of my newfound energy into my athletes and become a winning coach.

The next day, in front of the entire staff at Shawnigan, I announced my decision to retire from competitive rowing, as I referred to it. When I actually heard my words, the full magnitude of what my decision meant struck me for the first time. This was it. I was now not only done with rowing, but I was giving up on my dream of winning my Olympic gold medal—my obsession for so long—something that had affected every life decision I had made in the past decade. At the age of 25, long before my physical prime, and without ever realizing my dream, I was letting it go. Understandably, my voice was a little shaky.

After I sat down, a number of the staff wished me well, saying that the decision must have been difficult. They were kind gestures that assured me I wasn't alone. If only I had been willing to talk about it, no doubt I would have had many supportive listeners. But I didn't. Instead, I told everyone that, because I now had extra time on my hands, I was available to help wherever I was needed.

4 ▰▬▬▬▬▬

LIFE WITHOUT TRAINING

Don Rolston, the art teacher at Shawnigan, a kind and soft-spoken man with a passion for the arts, was the first to take me up on my offer. Knowing I had a background in visual arts, he asked me to come by the art room during class time and work with his students. My only hesitation was that it had been a long time since I had been a practising artist. Even though I knew one day my vocation would involve something to do with my interest in visual art, I hadn't given it much attention for a number of years.

I agreed to take Don up on his offer and soon found myself spending more and more time in the art room, working with other students or working on my own projects. It was great to be drawing again, creating something with my hands that was pleasing to the eye. It felt good to be finding success with something—anything.

When I wasn't in the classroom or on the lake coaching, I spent a lot of my time running and thinking. Coupled with a few visits to the weight room each week, I felt strong and healthy, but coming off of training four to six hours a day meant that I now had to watch my caloric intake. I had been burning 5,000-plus calories a day just training, and the food that was required to replenish that was immense. Now, not burning up all those calories, I had to be careful not to eat too much—something I wasn't used to.

I knew it was only a matter of time before my athletes would ask me why I'd quit training. When they did, I simply said that it was time, and they left it at that. I figured they were the last ones who needed to know about what I had been going through. I wanted their introduction to rowing to be positive. I also wanted their training to be as hard for them as it had for me when I was their age, so I put them through many of the same intense work-outs that Neil had put me through. At first, as I had with Neil, they thought I was crazy, but as they began to notice their fitness and boat speed improving, they embraced the added work as part of the necessary price for improving their chances of winning.

It was late March and my parents were flying out for a visit. I hadn't told them about quitting and because I wanted to get it over with fast I told them the news at dinner on our first night together. To my surprise I didn't struggle once with my announcement, but to my horror my parents seemed relieved. I wasn't thrilled to hear my dad say he was glad I was "finally getting on with my life." He didn't see how rowing could "pay the bills" and reminded me that if I competed in Barcelona, I would be 28 years old and without a degree or any other sort of possible career training. He was worried that I wasn't concerned enough about my plans for life after row-ing. As usual, he was right—I hadn't thought about any of that. I had been single-mindedly going after my Olympic gold medal and everything else was being ignored, but I had quit rowing because I was done, not because I wanted a job.

We sat in silence, intently eating our dinner until finally my Mom seemed to be struggling to say something. Then, like a solid right hook, out it came, "I'm glad you're retiring, Jason."

I stopped eating.

"You've been so angry about your rowing. It's like you've had something to prove—some unfinished business, perhaps. It hasn't been easy to be around you at times."

I sat for a moment not knowing what to say to Mom's perfect analysis of my situation. As always, she was bang on. I really had no reason to be surprised—she was my mom and that's what moms do: they look after, look out for, and protect their children. I was 25, but I was still her child—her youngest. She knew me inside and out, but I'd thought I had kept my demons hidden from everyone.

"It hasn't been easy, Mom."

"What hasn't been?"

"Losing."

"What do you mean, losing?"

Dad was still quiet. I'm sure he figured this was Mom's territory and there was no way he was going to venture into this conversation.

"Losing in Seoul. It's been hard."

"It was a race—you lost. I know it meant a lot to you, but life goes on. You have to let that go."

My heart began to race and my head started to spin as that sick feeling of losing in Seoul came back. I felt like everyone in the restaurant had heard what she had said and were now looking at me and waiting to hear what I had to say for myself. I felt exposed, like a little boy who'd been caught lying. I had been telling the world that everything was fine, while in fact things weren't fine, they were far from fine—I was broken, badly.

"I knew we should've talked about it when you got home from Seoul. We just left you alone knowing you didn't want to discuss it, and that was wrong. We should've made you talk. Jason, you can't just keep things inside of you."

I acknowledged Mom's comment and then quickly changed the topic. I couldn't remember the last time I had cried in front of my parents but I wasn't about to do it in a restaurant. After Mom and Dad flew home, I called my sister and brothers. Scott and Wendy said they understood and wished me well with my coaching. Paul, on the other hand, was mad that I was quitting.

"Big mistake, Jase. Don't do it. Just take some time off and get back in the game. It'll be worth it. Spracklen will turn that program around and it *will* be worth hangin' in there for Barcelona. Trust me—don't quit! Not yet. You're too young and you haven't seen your best days."

I heard him but I didn't want to listen. I knew that things being better in Barcelona was possible, but what it would take to get there was beyond me now. If I continued along the path that I had been on before I quit, I would end up in a hospital, and not for a physical ailment. Paul had no idea about the internal process I was using and the demons it had manifested. I had made up my mind and I didn't want to hear what Paul had to say—his honesty wasn't helping. I knew I was done, and that was that.

At the beginning of the spring term, Peter Yates put an entry form for the Canadian National Rowing Championships in my mailbox. The notion of travelling back to St. Catharines for Schoolboy's, as it was also known, was something I hadn't entertained. I tried to think of an event that would best suit the boys. The age categories on the West Coast didn't match the eastern schools at the time because Ontario still had Grade 13. If we did enter an event it would have to be a combination of senior and junior athletes. Also, we would have to train outside of the regular time allotted for rowing because it would be hard to combine the two programs without disrupting crews that had already been established.

I decided on the junior lightweight coxed four event, which meant that the athletes would be 16 years of age or younger and weigh in at 155 pounds or less, except the coxie, who would have to weigh at least 110 pounds. We selected the crew and tried to unify the lineup as best we could in the short time before we left.

Going back home to a regatta that had meant so much to me as a young boy wasn't without mixed emotions. As a 12-year-old, not only had I learned how to row in the St. Catharines Rowing Club's

Summer Camp program, but I had also spent four years rowing there in high school. My brothers and sister had rowed there too. My dad had rowed on the course and his dad before him. The place had a lot of history and memories for our family. Its most recent history for me was the summer of 1988 and our Olympic preparation. We had trained every day, twice a day, up and down the murky waters of the Old Welland Canal.

After a long day's travel, we made our way through the streets of Port Dalhousie until we eventually arrived on Henley Island. I walked down to the enormous dock that sat in front of the boathouse where all of the crews launched and docked their boats. Looking out over the course, I could see there were already dozens of crews out for their morning training sessions. There was a familiar buzz about the place. The lines of triangular streaming plastic flags were up and flapping in the wind. When we were in high school and those flags went up, it signified that Schoolboy's was coming and with that our chance to race—our chance to win.

My crew underperformed in their first race. I knew they were in a tough situation given how young and inexperienced they were for the age category, but Neil had always had us race older crews when I was at Ridley, and more often than not we won. Neil had never been one to make excuses when we underperformed. He would simply say we needed to work harder, and we did. I did the same with my crew; I kept the bar high and expected them to perform well in the semi-final and advance to the final.

On the day of their semi, standing on the shore watching them go by in fourth place I was surprised. I was also mad. They were better than this—fourth in the semi? Meeting them at the dock, I didn't have much to say. I asked how things went, to which they said, "Okay, I guess."

What? Okay? What the does that mean? What does okay mean? That you raced your best and still managed to lose? You didn't race okay—if you had, you would have advanced to the final. You should be more pissed off that you lost.

The way I saw it they weren't disappointed enough about having just lost their race. I didn't understand their lack of anger and frustration. With our chariot washed and put away, we watched the rest of the regatta as spectators.

We arrived back on the coast on Monday night. First thing the next morning, I headed to the woods for a long run. I had calmed down a bit and managed to find some perspective regarding our performance at Schoolboy's. I had always rowed as a heavyweight, but I realized that the lightweight event was tougher than I had originally thought. I had good friends who were lightweights and I'd always respected their ability to make weight and still perform exceptionally well. I knew that most lightweights had a reputation for having a lot of horsepower crammed into a small body. I'd understood that the lightweight division was very competitive, but I'd really had no idea just how competitive until this race.

When the rowers all weigh essentially the same, there are minute details that will distinguish the faster crew. Things like fitness and technique become paramount. If the crews also max out at a similar power-to-weight ratio, then races are bound to be closer and more competitive—it only makes sense. To win you need four athletes who are fitter, tougher and technically better than any of the other teams.

With a new appreciation of what it would take to win that event, I thought of all of things I would do differently the next time; but, when I thought of all the things I wanted to accomplish in my life, I realized that I didn't want to be an art teacher or a coach. As much as I had enjoyed being in the classroom and working with the students, I wanted to make more money than either one of those professions garnered. Having grown up in the home of a lifelong teacher, I saw how hard my dad had worked and how little he had been paid. That wasn't in my future—no way—so at the end of the school year, I packed all of my worldly possessions into three full suitcases and moved to Vancouver.

My new plan was to try my hand at advertising design. It was what I had studied at Syracuse University before I transferred to the University of Victoria to train with the national team, and I had loved it. I found the notion of trying to influence someone's purchasing or emotions with images and text interesting. I figured I would move back, show my portfolio around and be working within a few weeks.

What quickly became apparent was that my lack of experience in the workplace was going to be more of an obstacle than I had originally thought. I was 26 and I had never had a real job. I had a decent portfolio, knew I could work hard and was keen as hell, but I struggled just to get interviews.

It was hard to accept. When I was rowing, I'd belonged to an elite group of individuals. There were maybe a hundred people in the world, just a handful in Canada, who could do what I could do in a boat. There was a certain pride that came with that: an undeniable confidence. Now, having handed in my membership, I was no longer anything special. There was nothing of distinction that separated me from the rest. I was just an average person looking for an average job to pay bills. Eventually, my finances became so tight that I just had to find work—any work! I desperately needed someone to see some potential in me, and when I couldn't even land a job waiting tables, I was very discouraged.

It was late November 1990 and I had been invited to Shawnigan Lake School for a visit. I had nothing going on in Vancouver that weekend, so I jumped on a bus and caught the ferry over to the Island and went up to the school. It was great to be back. I saw some of the guys I had coached the year before—they were excited to see me. Everywhere I went on campus, I ran into people who seemed genuinely happy that I had come back for a visit.

"How's Vancouver? How's your design stuff going?" was the question I was getting from most of the staff. They weren't simply being polite; they were sincerely interested in how I was managing.

"Awful!" was what I wanted to say. Instead, I smiled and said that things were fine, a familiar response that I didn't recognize as being anything significant at the time.

Then I ran into the headmaster, Simon Bruce-Lockhart, who also asked how things were going. Simon was a family friend who had taught at Ridley with my dad. In fact, my dad had taught him when he attended the school during the 1960s. He had known me since the day I was born and, therefore, took a little extra interest in how things were going for me. Simon was a big man; he had played hockey, football and rugby while at Ridley. He also had a gentleness and kindness about him that allowed me to trust him with the truth.

I gave him the straight goods. I said things weren't going as well as I had hoped. I told him that I didn't have a job and was finding living in Vancouver very challenging. He said that I could always come back to Shawnigan and continue coaching rowing and working in the art room with Don. He told me to think about it and let him know. At first, I thought there was no way I was going to go back. That would be admitting defeat, and I was determined to make things work in Vancouver. All I needed was for someone to give me a chance.

When I started to think about the opportunity to go back to St. Catharines and win, I started to entertain the notion of accepting Simon's offer more seriously. If I went back, I could take the same group of athletes, who were now older, stronger and able to train harder, to win a national championship. That was an exciting possibility for me and, after some reflection, I accepted. Given that there were only a few weeks left until the Christmas break, I planned to arrive back for the beginning of the second term. I phoned Darby and told him my plans. He suggested I come home and work for him in the meantime. That would allow me to have Christmas with my family, earn some money and spend some time with my friends there before I started back at Shawnigan.

Darby had transitioned from rowing life to work life very well. His tremendous work ethic and ability to focus were suited perfectly to his construction business. He didn't do a lot of talking; he just made things happen. He offered to pay for my flight, gave me a place to sleep and put me to work. After paying him back for the airline ticket, anything else I earned would be for me. I figured the arrangement was more than fair, not to mention extremely generous so I took him up on it. On a cold morning in early December, back in St. Catharines, I grabbed a garbage bag, bent down and started cleaning up a frozen construction site.

Not being used to the cold winter weather after my years on the West Coast, I struggled to get warm. Picking up used Styrofoam coffee cups and empty chip bags in sub-freezing temperatures had me reflecting on my life goals. A year ago I'd been training full-time for one of the most coveted sporting prizes in the world. My life had purpose and I was excited to be chasing something so distinguished. Now I was picking up someone else's trash. "What doesn't kill me . . ."—isn't that how it goes? Yes, this was a new low for sure, but it gave me a reminder of what I didn't want in life and that, if I intended to achieve my goals, I had better get my proverbial shit together—quickly.

In the spring term, my job was to work with the senior lightweights. Even though they were in Grade 11 and 16 years old, they would still qualify for the junior event in which we had failed to make the final the previous year. Three of the guys from the junior coxed four were back, and when I announced on the first day that our goal for this year's program was to return to St. Catharines and win the event we had lost the previous year, the returning members seemed more than ready. They seemed hungrier this time—like they had developed a little more fight. When one of them referred to this trip as a chance for revenge, I knew they were ready to do things properly this time.

All I needed was one more rower and a coxie. Initially it wasn't apparent who that would be. I needed some time to watch the guys in action and get a sense of what made them tick—why they chose to row. So much of what makes a successful crew, or any team for that matter, is the chemistry of the combined individuals. It isn't all about raw talent. In my first year at Syracuse University, I was a part of a freshman crew that would've made any coach drool—even *Sports Illustrated* ranked us as their number one pick that year.

Three of us were from Ridley, four were top rowers from the States, and the last guy was a novice walk-on. Through the early part of the season we won all the time, every weekend destroying top university crews, but by the end of the season, the other universities had gained experience, and we were hard pressed to find such easy victories. Ultimately, at the IRA (National) Championships that year, we came second to Princeton in a race we should have won. Looking back, I realized that we'd had the talent, but not the chemistry. There were too many chiefs, me being one of them, so we never bonded as a crew. Each of us was rowing for himself, not for the others—the kiss of death.

Now, as a coach, I knew that it was important to have bodies but equally important that they felt they belonged to something bigger. I had three guys who'd competed the previous year. They were perfect for the job and they all filled important roles. Our strokeman was the best technician in the crew—he was strong, tenacious and, most importantly, smart. He knew how to race and how to feel the boat. Guys like him didn't come along too often.

The two others were focused and serious at times, yet playful in their own bizarre ways. What I admired most about both of them was that they could push themselves harder than any high school rowers I had ever coached—they were both boat movers. What we didn't have was a firecracker—a guy who would say the perfect unscripted thing at the just the right moment to cut tension or unite a crew. We needed what every great crew had, someone who was a little crazy—but good crazy. I just had to find one.

There was a Grade 8 boy named Bryce who was tiny and perfect for the job as coxie, but he was young and had no experience. He reminded me of Tim Coy the first year he coxed us at Ridley. Tim was young and inexperienced too, but he ended up the winningest Canadian high school athlete ever. Based on my experience with Tim, I decided to take a chance with Bryce. With my strokeman being so good, I figured it would be hard for Bryce to screw up. I made arrangements for him to train with us during the senior time slot. One seat filled—one to go.

That one turned out to be David, a boy who was constantly getting into trouble and seemed to be in with the wrong crowd. His housemaster felt he needed the challenge that rowing might provide—a more productive focus for his mischievous energy.

I was familiar with Dave's reputation, but thought he was a good guy, harmless really—just a little rough around the edges. He was also the perfect size for lightweight and, from what I had heard, a fierce competitor on the rugby field. That night I asked Dave if he'd be interested in coming out to rowing the next day. He looked at me as if I was crazy, and in the background his snickering roommate let me know he thought it was an absurd notion too.

Some teenagers have an uncanny ability of saying everything they're thinking without uttering a sound. Dave's unspoken response to me was, "To hell with you buddy. Loser." He took pride in his reputation on the rugby pitch and clearly wasn't about to relinquish that for a shot at a rowing crew—losers rowed, not tough guys like him.

"Okay. No problem," I replied. "But if you're as tough as you think you are, come down to the boathouse tomorrow and find out."

"Yeah, I'll think about it," was my cue to leave.

I did, but on my way out I said, "Dress warmly."

The next day, as I had hoped, Dave showed up. After I got my boating order sorted out, I walked over to him and said, "Change of heart?"

"Maybe."

"I'm glad you came."

He shrugged. I put him on an ergometer (a machine designed to replicate the motion of rowing). I showed him some basic technique and then left him to figure out the rest on his own. I went off to see how the others were doing and when I returned he was managing just fine. Neil had always told us that coaches created lousy rowers. He believed the motion of rowing was natural and that, if given the chance, anyone could row properly.

"Try a little more pressure for a couple of strokes."

On the next stroke, the speedometer displayed some decent numbers.

"Harder," I said.

He looked at me incensed. He bore down and started pulling harder. Immediately, each consecutive stroke produced a better score.

"Okay. That's enough. Grab your stuff and come with me." I went out to join the other crew members as they were about to head out onto the lake for the workout. I gave them instructions for the warm-up as they rowed away and then went to grab my winter clothes.

You can keep quite warm rowing on a cold day in February on the West Coast, but you get damn cold sitting in a coach boat not moving a single muscle. I started my outboard engine, which on a day like this could be a challenge, and motioned for Dave to get in. I threw him a lifejacket and said, "Put this on and have a seat up front."

After about 30 minutes of watching the crew go through their warm-up, I asked my new recruit if he thought he could do that.

"Sure. I think so."

"Let's find out."

I picked up my megaphone and told Bryce to stop the boat. I asked the guy in three-seat to undo his shoes so Dave could have a try. I knew three-seat was his best shot. In an eight-oared shell, if a coach wanted to hide someone who wasn't as experienced as the others, that was the place.

I showed Dave how to hold onto the oar and a few other basic things that would, at the very least, ensure he didn't get catapulted from the boat. I had the stern four (back half) row on their own, while the bow four (foward half) set up, or balanced, the boat. This allowed Dave, sitting in the bow section, to get a feel for the boat moving under him. After a series of progressive stroke drills it was his turn to try.

Once Dave looked comfortable enough to pull up the training wheels, I told Bryce to get all eight rowing. I followed along to see how Dave would manage. Within a few moments I could see that he was going along just fine. In fact, I was hard-pressed to find any major technical issues with his stroke.

I picked up my megaphone and ordered Bryce to do a few tens (power strokes). Then I said to Dave, "Just relax and hang on. The boat is going to pick up a little speed. Don't panic and don't try too hard. Just increase your pressure as you feel more comfortable with each stroke."

Dave managed each ten without any major problems. I decided to get our strokeman to push a little harder. "Okay, Nick, knock the rate up a bit and let's see how she goes."

Again, Dave did surprisingly well. Sure, he looked a little rough, and his motion wasn't as naturally fluid as some of the others, but that would come. Hell, this was his first time rowing ever and he was holding his own beautifully.

With our racing season looming, I decided to push Dave a little more. "Okay, we'll do one more piece, Bryce—Nick, crank it up!"

I knew that if he was going to blow up, it was going to be on this piece. Sure enough, half way through, Dave tensed up, caught a crab (unable to remove or release the oar blade from the water, which results in the blade acting like a brake) and was thrown back against the boy behind him. As the boat came to a stop, Dave sat up and struggled to get himself back into position.

"You okay?" I asked.

He looked at me, smiling, and said, "Yup."

Back on the dock, after the boat and oars had been put away, I called Dave over and asked him, "So how was that?"

He gave me a satisfied grin, "Awesome."

We had just found our fourth guy.

For the remainder of the season, I had my eight row as two coxed fours head-to-head during practice time as often as I could. By the time we arrived at Henley Island for the Canadian National Rowing Championships, we were the fastest crew on the West Coast in our category. I was focused on doing everything I could as a coach to ensure these guys did their best—which for me, meant winning. As much as I knew my crew wanted to win, I too wanted to win—badly.

On the day of the finals we found ourselves in lane three with the fastest qualifying time. We washed our boat and tried to stay relaxed. As racing shells went, ours was by no means the newest boat in the final, but I always reminded my rowers of what Neil used to tell us, "It's not the chariot, it's the horses pulling it." I knew one thing for sure, we had some good horses, and they were eager to come busting out of the gates.

Forty minutes before our race was called, I huddled the crew around our shining chariot and reminded them of our talk that morning—this race was a war, and we hadn't come all this way to lose. They were going out there to do whatever it took to ensure they won. I knew they understood that; they'd certainly heard it enough from me over the past five months.

With 30 minutes to go until the start of our race, the event was announced over the loudspeaker. "Remember to get out front and stay there," I said. "No matter what it takes. Bryce, don't be afraid to put the whips to them in the last 500. Okay? Let's go."

Traditionally, lightweight rowers and coxies were required to weigh in the morning of their event. That morning we came down to the Island and lined up to do just that. I was a big believer in having true lightweights, meaning that at any time during the year they could weigh in and meet the weight restriction for their event. I didn't believe in athletes training 5 or 10 pounds above weight all year long and then sweating down in the final weeks leading up to the championships. Not only was starving themselves unhealthy for their young bodies, it also compromised their performance. I preferred a boat of rested athletes with full tanks over one that hadn't eaten properly and had been running all morning to sweat off the last few ounces of water weight.

The night before we had been to an all-you-can-eat pasta restaurant and then to a favourite local ice cream place for dessert. These guys had pigged out and, as I looked around at the other crews weighing in, I knew we were the only ones that had. Sure, we gave up some height and size with that strategy, but I figured in the last 500 metres of the race, some of that triple-decker, peanut butter, double fudge would pay off.

Bryce, on the other hand, had not eaten enough. He was underweight, which meant he would have to carry added weight in the boat to reach the required 110 pounds that each coxie had to weigh. It wasn't ideal to have stagnant weight, but it wasn't worth fretting over either.

Shoving them off for the final, I was more nervous than I had been the previous year. These guys were favoured to win, and a loss would reflect poorly on me as their coach. I wasn't prepared for that.

I paced around nervously for about 25 minutes until it was time to meet up with my old Ridley gang on the bank of the course to watch the race.

They were my best friends: Dave Walker, Darby Berkhout, John Walker and Kevin O'Brien. As I watched my crew come by the Island at the 1,300-metre mark, they were comfortably out front.

"Hey, Skeet. They got it," Darby said quietly. There were only a handful of people who referred to me as Skeet, a nickname I had inherited from my dad, and all of them were standing there with me.

I wasn't ready to celebrate just yet. In rowing, anything could happen—broken equipment, a crab, any of which could change the outcome of a race with only metres remaining.

Finally, we heard the bang. BANG, again. From the Island you couldn't see the finish line so you had to wait for the announcer to tell you who had won. I stood there, my heart pounding, thinking those gunshots were closer than they should have been. Someone must have moved back on them. *Come on! Come on! Announce the winner!*

Then, the same voice that used to announce my victories from the same old speakers atop a few telephone poles came, "The results of event number nine—the junior lightweight coxed four. First place—Shawnigan Lake School."

They had done it. I had done it.

When we arrived back in Shawnigan, there wasn't anyone in sight. "You'd think someone would've come out to say hello," Dave said, disappointed. "Is it true that the entire school at Brentwood comes out to greet their rowers? And that they get off of their bus and walk through a long line of crossed oars while everyone cheers?"

"Look," I said. "You didn't do this for a cheer rally. You did this for yourself. This wasn't about Shawnigan or your parents or your friends or anybody other than you. All of the training you went through, the race this past weekend—all of it will stay with you forever; you'll never forget these last few days—ever."

They all smiled. Deep down, they knew that was true. They had done this for themselves and each other—and that was enough.

Quitting rowing had been the best decision I could have made. Not only had I enjoyed my time coaching, but I had also enjoyed my time in the classroom. I had grown to appreciate why my dad taught and, as cliché as it may sound, I'd begun to feel that I was making a positive difference in the lives of young people. I decided to go back to university and finish my degree in visual arts and then get my education degree. It was going to take a number of years, but I was prepared to invest the necessary time.

I enrolled at UVic and rented a room in a beautiful house down by the beach, not too far from the university. I even had a social life, something that I hadn't been used to as a full-time athlete. I also stumbled upon a new sport that suited my personality perfectly. During the previous year at Shawnigan, I had started training for an ultra-marathon. But this one was a little different—it was called the Knee Knacker, a 30-mile trail run that covered the Baden Powell Trail in the North Shore mountains of Vancouver. The elevation change during the run was 16,000 feet: 8,000 feet up and 8,000 feet down.

The training was great—hours and hours of long steady running through picturesque forests. Seoul was now almost three years behind me, and as much as my rowing nightmares were less frequent, unfortunately other demons had shown up. My obsession with winning had been replaced by my obsession with something else—my body. I couldn't control winning a gold medal, but I could control how I looked. I began to monitor the amount of food that I ate and the amount of exercise that I got each day. With each passing week, as I lost weight, I saw the results of something that I was controlling. Everything was about finishing the day having burned more calories than I had consumed. That meant lots of running, and lots of rice cakes and V8 juice. On those occasions when I found myself stuffing my face with too much food, I simply ate close to nothing the next day and did extra workouts. That accomplished two things: I kept my weight down and I punished myself for being weak by not controlling my cravings. I never got to the point of becoming bulimic, but I was certainly not well—physically, mentally or emotionally.

It was a strange situation for me. The logical, rational side of my brain understood that I was doing something unhealthy and ultimately dangerous—the blood in my urine after long runs confirmed that, but I refused to change my behaviour. Many days I convinced myself that losing weight would allow me to gain back the self-respect I had lost in Seoul. I just wasn't ready to acknowledge the root cause of this crazy, irrational behaviour, fearing it would be far more confusing and painful than what I was doing to myself.

Toward the end of my first year in art school, one of my professors, an older gentleman whom I respected, asked me an unusual question. "Why are you here, Jason?" He wasn't trying to be deep or philosophical. What he meant was, "Why are you studying at this particular university?" His point was simply that my work was detailed, graphic and commercial. He suggested that my talents might be better served in a graphic design program like the one at the Emily Carr College of Art + Design in Vancouver.

That summer I moved back to the mainland. I was excited about going to this new school. Emily Carr had a good reputation, and it was located in a beautiful setting on Granville Island in the heart of the city. I had to attend a portfolio review, during which two instructors asked me some simple questions about my work while they looked closely at my slides. When all of their questions were answered, they said I should hear from them soon. By mid-July, I received a letter from them indicating that my application had been accepted.

My living arrangements were simple to say the least. I was sleeping on a couch at my friends Pat and Trev's place. I had known Pat Turner for a long time. He was a member of the Canadian men's eight that won the gold medal in Los Angeles in 1984. It was weird: Pat had been a hero of mine when I was a teenager, and now we were roommates.

Trev Neufeld had been a friend of Pat's since their early years at UBC. Trev was crazy, but fun crazy—always a blast to be around and eager to share a laugh. He was also one of the friendliest individuals I had ever met. He was as interesting to listen to as he was interested in finding out about others. I was always amazed at his ability to engage in conversations with such a diverse group of people. Living with these two was the best thing that could have happened to me at the time. They were a lot of fun, but they were also the "kid gloves" I desperately needed. They provided me with quiet and subtle guidance. As for my social life, Hannah, one of our downstairs neighbours, and I were romantically involved.

By the end of July 1992, the Barcelona Olympics were well underway. As the halfway point of the games neared, so did the final of the men's eight. The race was always held on the second Sunday of the Olympics, and this year I planned to be as far away from TVs and newspapers as possible. Deep down I didn't want Canada to win. Even though I knew all of the guys on the crew, I wanted them to lose. They'd placed second at the previous year's World Championships and were certainly capable of winning in Barcelona, but I wanted them to get killed. If I couldn't have a gold medal, neither could they. Call it childish, cowardly, selfish—call it whatever you want, but it was the honest truth.

Although Hannah knew how angry I was about my race in Seoul, she didn't understand the full scope of that anger and about the demons that had been haunting me. She suggested we go on a camping trip down on the coast of Oregon. The plan was to go to

Cannon Beach, hang out there for a few days and enjoy the beautiful sights. Neither of us said it, but we both knew the real reason for this trip was for me to hide from the race.

The drive down through Oregon was stunning. The US Pacific Northwest has some of the most picturesque landscapes in the world. The weather was ideal. It didn't rain. It wasn't too hot. We couldn't have asked for anything better. We went on some great bike rides, took beautiful runs along the beach and cooked some terrific meals. But despite the scenery, the company and the relaxation, all I could think about was the final of the men's eight.

As I awoke on the morning of Sunday, August 2, my first thought was that the race was over. The 1992 Olympic champions had been awarded their gold medals and were probably well into their celebrations by now. How had it played out? Had Canada won or had the defending champions taken the gold again—the Germans, who I thought had stolen the gold from me in 1988?

That morning, on our way home, Hannah and I stopped in at a little mom-and-pop grocery store in a small town in western Oregon. There was a decrepit *USA Today* stand by the entrance to the store with a few papers left in it. I wanted so badly to look, but I told myself, *Don't do it, Jase—you're down here to have fun. Don't ruin it!* As Hannah and I walked around the store gathering some items for dinner, I could sense the newspaper taunting me. One quick look and I would know the results. I resisted the urge, but with each passing moment my anxiety grew. I paid for our groceries and promptly walked toward the exit. I couldn't help myself any longer. As we passed the newsstand, I glanced down at the paper. There was no mention of rowing, but that only meant that the US team hadn't won. If they had, the news would have been splashed all over the front page.

As soon as I walked into the house later that afternoon, Pat came out of his room to greet me. "Did you hear the news?" he asked.

My heart was pounding and my hands were sweating as I waited for him to speak.

"They did it. Spracklen's boys won the gold."

"Get out! Really?"

"Yup!"

I smiled as best as I could, then quickly turned and walked out of the room. I had to get out of the house. I didn't want Pat to see how disappointed I was. Knowing that I should have been ashamed for the way I felt didn't make the feeling any less real—I was pissed off that they had won. As I walked back down the stairs, Hannah took one look at me and knew that something was wrong.

"What happened?"

"They won," I answered.

Repeatedly circling the backyard in disbelief, I felt as though I was going to throw up. I tried to relax and breathe; I couldn't be sick in front of these guys. Eventually I was able to calm myself down and the nausea subsided. I rejoined Hannah and helped her unpack the car to begin airing out all of our camping stuff. With that done, I knew there was only one thing that would help me process this startling news. I put on my running shoes and took off for the trails.

I can't believe it. My worst nightmare has come true. Andy, John and all of the other guys are now Olympic gold medallists. It couldn't be true. Paul was right. I shouldn't have quit. I should've kept going. I could've rowed for three more years. What a pussy I was to quit. If I had kept at it, I'd be celebrating my gold medal in Barcelona right now. You loser! Look at what you did.

I had never experienced anger like this before—especially not toward myself. Every muscle in my body was at the ready, on fire. My thoughts were spitting rage. If there had been another of me standing there, I would've torn him apart with my bare hands and enjoyed it.

The nausea came back as my head began to spin. I stopped running and started walking instead. My breathing quickened—faster and faster until I was heaving to suck in enough air to prevent myself from passing out. At that moment one thought struck me like a speeding train: how was I going to congratulate any of the guys in the Canadian crew knowing that I'd hoped that the Germans or anyone else would beat them? Tears started to run down my face, and my breathing became more spastic as I sobbed uncontrollably beneath the giant evergreens. I stopped walking, put my hands to my head and squatted down. I tried desperately to regain my composure before another runner or hiker ventured along and saw me.

Then, from deep within my core, came a burst of rage that produced the loudest scream I'd ever known.

A few weeks later, our entire house was invited to a party to celebrate the Canadian rowers' victory. I had no choice but to go. How could I not? There was no feasible excuse. These were friends of mine; I couldn't exactly say, "I'm really sorry, but I'm not happy that you won." Not without coming off like a complete jerk. The house was packed with young people excited to have a reason to join in the party. Walking into the sea of twentysomethings that filled the living room, I spotted John. He noticed me at the exact same time and I smiled. He returned the smile, but his look was gentle. His eyes were soft and acknowledging. They said, "Yeah, I won a gold medal, but there's a side of me that understands how you're feeling about that." I instantly felt better about our meeting. I walked up to him, extended my hand in congratulations and meant it.

"Thanks, Jase," he said. "Thanks a lot."

"Winning must have felt good," I said.

"It did. It felt really good."

"Well, you deserve it, John. I'm happy for you."

No sooner had I digested that moment than I ran into Mike, another member of the crew. We'd been at training camps together but had never raced for Canada in the same crew. When I shook his hand, I could tell Mike was well into another night of celebrating his Olympic victory.

"Hey, Jase man, thanks. It was a blast. Whoooweee! I tell ya what, Jase. You shouldn't have quit. You would've loved rowing for Spracklen. His training was hard core, just the way you like it, man. It was so intense."

I didn't need to hear that—not any if it. Thankfully, we were interrupted by another well-wisher who was more up to speed than I was with the number of libations Mike had consumed. It was the perfect opportunity to escape.

It's not that I was mad at Mike—how could I be? He hadn't meant any harm by what he'd said; he was just being honest. He was right, though. I would have loved rowing for Spracklen. Under normal circumstances, I would've thrived on the challenge of his training sessions, but the past four years had been anything but normal circumstances.

That night, my Olympic dream finally ended and I thought, *Now what? Who was I if I wasn't an Olympic gold medallist?* More importantly, for my own well-being, what could I achieve that would fill the giant hole that my Olympic disappointment had created? I enjoyed my art, but I didn't lie awake at night thinking about it. It was just something that I did, something that came easily to me. Where was the reward in that? I needed something difficult to chase again. Something that people would notice. Something that would make them say, "Wow! Did you see what he just did?"

I wanted to achieve something, be somebody. I remembered the summer I had accepted a job as camp counsellor aboard a tall ship sailing from San Francisco to Kona on the Island of Hawaii and then on to Victoria. The trip was memorable for two reasons. One was that I got seasick just hours out of the harbour and had to depend on ginger root capsules to get me through it. The other was an incident that happened on the way back to Victoria.

I was having an afternoon nap when I was awakened by a loud thump that came from above my cabin ceiling. Sarah, one of the students, had fallen from the crow's nest and lay on the deck. Our camp director, who was also the nurse, was beside her doing an inspection of her injuries.

As I knelt down beside Sarah, I could see that she was indeed badly hurt, which was no surprise since she had fallen eight storeys and landed on a steel deck. Her shinbones had ripped through the skin just above her ankles, her hips looked uneven, and her head was scraped and bruised. We could only imagine how bad the internal damage was.

Moments later the captain informed us that three shipping vessels had answered his mayday call and were steaming toward us. Good news at this point since, other than painkillers, we had no facilities aboard.

Within 20 minutes there was a roar from off the stern that was louder than anything I had ever heard. It was a Navy Hurricane jetfighter sent out to determine the distance between the aircraft carrier USS *Abraham Lincoln* and us, and whether a rescue helicopter could make a return trip safely. Soon after, the thumping sound of a helicopter was audible as it made its way toward us from the same direction as the Hurricane. I had never seen a military helicopter in real life; it was impressive. It circled us and eventually came to a stop off the port side, where it hovered about 30 feet above the ocean. We stood at the ship's railing and watched as a Navy Seal jumped out of the helicopter without any hesitation. He disappeared for a moment under the water's surface. Moments later he hit the ship's ladder with the precision of a guided missile.

He grabbed our stretcher and motioned for me and another counsellor to help gently move Sarah onto it. As slowly as we could, trying to be careful with each small movement, we secured her to the flimsy old stretcher. From there we carried her to the stern of the boat where the helicopter was now lowering a caged stretcher that would lift Sarah off the ship. As quickly as we could, we tied her into the suspended metal bed. Then the Navy Seal signalled for the helicopter to begin hoisting Sarah off the ship. The Seal asked me to assist him in holding onto one of the two ropes that hung from the caged stretcher.

"Hold this as tightly as you can," he said. "If we don't, she'll start to spin like a windmill in the turbulence."

I grabbed my rope and wrapped it around my arm. Within seconds, Sarah was aboard and our Seal was now calmly moving toward the ship's ladder. I followed him closely. He turned, grabbed my hand again. "You take care."

With that, he turned and leapt toward the cold wavy waters that were now turning blue as the sun began to break through the clouds. He resurfaced and swam about 40 feet off the port side, stopped and looked up as a harness was arriving at his exact spot.

Once aboard he stuck his head out of the side door and gave a salute and a thumbs-up as the helicopter tilted forward and sped off. Everyone on the ship cheered.

Later that evening I walked slowly to the bow of the boat and sat down. There are people who fall eight feet and don't survive. What exactly did Sarah have left to do in her life that was so important that someone, something, decided that today wasn't her day to die? This was yet another reminder to live my days with purpose and appreciation. This goal I was in search of—the accomplishment that would fill my appetite for achieving—wasn't going to just show up. I had to go after it with the same tenacity I had with my Olympic dream.

5

NEW BEST FRIENDS

For me, Emily Carr was a great place to go to school. All of my instructors were superb. They were all working designers, which kept them current, relevant and interesting. The culture of the school was hardcore to say the least. The school was open until 3:00 AM every night. The workload was heavy, and our instructors' expectations were high. The students were competitive and driven.

My problem was that I wasn't ready to commit to that sort of competition. My ultra-marathons were different. They were safe because I was just too damn slow to ever win. I knew that if I pushed myself hard enough with my art, I could be among the top students, but what if I tried and wasn't? What if I lost again at something that I thought I could win? I wasn't ready for another fall like that. I knew how ugly things could get for me when winning something was on the line. I know my decision disappointed some of my instructors and a few of my classmates, but I could live with that. I couldn't live with losing out on some sort of prize or recognition after busting my ass for four years. My survival strategy for Emily Carr was to do just enough, and no more.

Later that winter Hannah and I were spending a weekend with friends on one of the Gulf Islands when we bumped into some parents of a student I had taught at Shawnigan. They had sailed over for the weekend from Vancouver—just the two of them and their dog, a beautiful golden retriever. I had always wanted another dog—in particular a golden—but my lifestyle hadn't, to that point, supported the notion of caring properly for one.

This golden was with the Canadian Guide Dogs for the Blind, and his people were called puppy walkers, meaning they were responsible for socializing him from the time he was eight weeks old until he was a year old, at which time he could be transferred to a school that would train him to be a guide dog. Their job entailed taking him to as many places as possible during their daily routine—restaurants, movies, grocery shopping, etc. It even meant that he travelled with them on airplanes, buses—pretty much any form of transportation. The whole point was to get him used to living in a city and experiencing as much city stuff as possible. That sounded awesome to me. The bonus was it didn't cost them a penny. They even had the dog's food provided free of charge. It sounded almost too good to be true, and it was: the catch was that you'd eventually have to give up the dog.

Hannah and I returned home the next day and I continued to think about that dog and about applying to be a puppy walker myself. I was convinced that if I kept the relationship like a job—strictly business—making sure I did not get emotionally attached, I would be fine. Besides, if I understood this correctly, it was sort of like a competition, in that whoever could do the best job socializing their dog, won. Well, I was up for that; I would make my puppy the best guide dog they had ever seen.

After a long conversation on the phone with Roberta, one of the organization's representatives, she decided that I might be suited for the job. A week later she came by to meet everyone and inspect the house. She was warm and kind, and I imagined her to be a great dog trainer—patient and loving. Thirty minutes into our conversation, we were discussing the pup that I would be matched with. I had passed; however, the litter would not be born until late April, which meant the puppy would not be ready to leave its mom until June. It was going to be a long wait.

Finally the day arrived. My ball of fluff was ready for me to bring home. His name was Ike. Playing in the front yard that evening, Ike attracted attention. The neighbours came out to meet the new addition to our house. As he bounded over the lawn from one person to the next, it became quite clear that he was one cute little guy. It occurred to me that the whole plan to keep Ike strictly business was going to be a little harder than I had originally thought.

Over the next few weeks, Ike continued growing—both physically and into the hearts of everyone in the house. Each weekend Pat, Trev and I would take him down to Granville Island where he would work his magic. By this time Hannah and I had gone our separate ways, but Ike was a living example of flypaper—attracting women everywhere he went. His beautiful blond, shiny coat, the flowing feathers on his chest and legs, and his adorable broad head all combined for one handsome pooch. He was incredible, and we certainly didn't mind answering the inevitable questions. How old is he? What's his name? Where did you get him? And so it went, on and on. We went everywhere together: restaurants, grocery stores, movies. His socializing was going well.

At the beginning of July, I began taking some classes at UBC. To earn my Bachelor of Design, I had to take a number of traditional academic courses first. When school started I showed up early for my first class and explained to the professor why I had this puppy, and that, if it was okay with him, he'd be joining us for the duration of the course. Technically he couldn't say no because guide dogs in training are afforded the same privileges as real guide dogs, but I figured it was a courtesy to ask and I knew, with Ike standing there beside me, no person with a pulse was going to be able to say no.

Sure enough, Ike was allowed to survey the course and, starting that day, he slept his way through six weeks of a Canadian physical geography class. In September, with the dean's permission, Ike also joined me for every class at Emily Carr. In no time at all he was adopted by all of my fellow classmates. As he got older and I occasionally left him at home with Pat or Trev, I would hear nothing but "Where's Ike?" for the entire day.

By Christmas Ike and I had become close, and the thought of giving him back in a few months seemed unimaginable. The "business" approach I had decided on for this temporary adoption had withered away. I was still determined to help him become an outstanding guide dog, but I was softening on some of the rules. I still had him walk on my left side only and made sure he stopped at all curbsides before we crossed. I even tried to discourage him from chasing cats and squirrels as best I could, but the "don't let him sleep on your bed" rule was out the door. Tiger had always slept at my feet, so one night when Ike put his chin on my bed and looked at me with his dark brown puppy-dog eyes, I decided to invite him up. He was a great bedmate. It was like having a huge hot-water bottle at the foot of the bed. On those cold and damp West Coast nights, despite his snoring, Ike was a welcome source of warm body heat.

I decided to take him home with me for Christmas. It turned out to be an easier process than I had originally thought. I just phoned the airline, told them that I was flying with a guide dog in training, and that was it. When I showed up for my flight, a flight attendant met me at the gate and put out her arm for me to take hold of. "No, I'm not blind," I said. "This little guy is only in training." She looked at me, a little embarrassed at first, and then she squatted down to give Ike a nice warm welcome. We travelled at the front of the plane so Ike would have room to stretch out. For the entire duration of the trip, the attendants spoiled us rotten.

My visit home that year was wonderful. Ike was a welcome novelty, and everyone who came by the house got a taste of what it was to know him. He was as charming as he had ever been, and aside from the huge dump he left in the living room the first night he arrived, he behaved perfectly.

My parents were smitten. My mom would say to me every day, "How on earth are you going to give him up?"

To be honest, I was trying not to think about that. All I knew was that my life was going along a heck of lot better than it had been in recent years and Ike was a huge reason why. Along with school, he required my constant attention—he was something I took care of. The result of that was that my rowing nightmares were becoming less frequent and my eating was better. I was certainly on the road to becoming a happier person.

The flight back wasn't as smooth as the flight out. Halfway to Vancouver, I smelled something that resembled apple juice but couldn't find where it was coming from. Then I noticed that Ike had woken up from a nap and was licking his belly. Looking down I saw that he was wet and the entire carpet around him was wet—Ike had peed himself in his sleep. I quickly pulled out a towel from my knapsack and began to pat dry the carpet. I was shocked. Ike had never had an accident in his sleep before. A week later I awoke to find the entire middle section of my bed completely soaked.

After a number of tests, including X-rays, and blood and urine samples, the vets discovered that Ike had been shortchanged on a few body parts. He only had one fully developed kidney; his bladder was too small, irregularly shaped and slightly in the wrong spot; and the sphincter that was supposed to prevent him from "leaking" when he slept wasn't working too well. That meant Ike was not fit to be a guide dog. He was removed from the program and offered to me as a pet—for a dollar.

Over the next few weeks, using medication, managing his water intake and ensuring he had a late-night pee before bed, we were able to control Ike's incontinence. The other issues, especially his kidney, were still uncertain. The vet said he could live one year, three years, five years, or a full life; there was no way of telling. It all depended on how long his one kidney was able to function and do the work of two.

I decided to keep him. It didn't matter if Ike was going to live one year or ten, I would make them great ones. I continued to take him to school with me every day. No one ever asked how the training was going. I'm guessing he had become so well known and liked that the powers that be simply accepted him as part of the school's culture. My classmates didn't mind; Ike was a welcome addition to our studios. At the beginning of every class he would make his rounds and say hello with his body wags and moans of appreciation.

Although I was living in Vancouver, my good friend Fiona in Victoria was forever trying to hook me up with other women. As much as I appreciated her being in my corner, to date she had struck out every time.

"Now, now, Mr. Have-no-faith-in-me. This time, I've done it—she's perfect," she said to me one day on the phone. "Robyn's a national team runner. She's going to be racing at the Commonwealth Games in a few weeks. She's beautiful. She's a redhead. She has a great sense of humour. She comes from a big family. And, if I do say so myself, she has gorgeous legs. Oh, and did I mention she's beautiful?" I agreed to meet Robyn at Cadboro Bay Beach, one of Victoria's many beautiful oceanside parks. Ike and I arrived early, and he decided the perfect throwing stick would help pass the time. Shortly after two o'clock, true to Fiona's words, a beautiful redhead with legs that said "I'm a serious runner" walked toward us.

With her hand outstretched she said, "You must be Jason?"

"You must be Robyn," I returned, as I stuck out my hand to meet hers.

I must have been a little overexcited because while delivering my intended firm handshake, I heard her wrist pop. *Oops—easy does it, big guy.* Not wanting to draw attention to my overzealous greeting, Robyn chose to ignore it—one point for her.

It was an absolutely beautiful August day with hardly a cloud in the sky. The hot sun, combined with the cool salty breeze coming off the ocean, made for the perfect temperature. There were families picnicking on the beach and children splashing in the water. A few hours into our date, things were going along perfectly. In fact, I had to admit that Fiona had outdone herself this time. Robyn was everything and more than I had been led to expect. Naturally, I began to concern myself with nailing the all-important second date.

I decided to show interest in her upcoming 3,000-metre race. The problem was that I was afraid that during the conversation I would give away my obsession with winning. I decided to tread lightly. "I hear you have a big race coming up next weekend. What do you think? Are you going to win it or what?"

After a long pause, she answered quietly, "I'm really not expecting much. I'm just going to go out there and give it my best shot and see what happens."

I couldn't believe my ears. *Give it your best shot? You've got to be kidding!* That was something you told a group of six-year-olds before a dodgeball game. I was dumbfounded. I expected this elite international track and field competitor to display confidence and bravado—like most of the elite runners I knew. Instead of telling me what I expected to hear—and, truth be told, what I wanted to hear was that she was going out there to win—I listened to a long, drawn-out list of excuses as to why she wasn't prepared. This was an international track race—the Commonwealth Games, for God's sake.

In my head I was creating my own version of why Robyn was so ill-prepared and how, as a result, she was going to fare in her upcoming event. At this stage of my life, if I was thinking it, I was probably going to say it, so I knew I needed to end this conversation quickly if I had any hope of landing that second date. Despite her unconventional racing strategy, she was beautiful, she was smart, she could run, and she had the body to prove it—what was not to like?

A week later I was back on the ferry to Victoria to watch Robyn's race. No blind date this time, just the race. I stayed with Fiona and she, of course, wanted all the details. Had I phoned Robyn? Sent her a letter? I confided that I had made a quick call to wish her luck in her race and sent along flowers. As far as I was concerned, given Robyn's expectations going into the race, she was going to need luck—desperately.

Arriving at the University of Victoria the afternoon of Robyn's race was a strange experience. Seeing all of the international athletes in their colourful tracksuits brought back memories of walking through the Olympic Village in 1988. As I walked through the crowd, I was reminded yet again that I was no longer an elite athlete—I had given up my membership. Instead, I was now one of the many thousands of spectators who had come to watch. In Seoul, local children would ask us for our autograph—not a big deal, but it did provide a reminder that there was some notoriety to our being there. Today, the local children of Victoria were approaching the athletes surrounding me and asking for their autographs—not mine. *Hey, suck it up, buddy—it was your choice to quit.*

Come race time, I realized how distinctly different track and field was to rowing. When we backed ourselves into the starting gates before a race, we were quiet and contemplative. There were usually no onlookers except for the officials and maybe a few coaches and it is generally only the last 300 metres—less than a quarter of the race—that spectators watch. By contrast, as the athletes in Robyn's race were paraded into the stadium, there was much fanfare. All of the runners stripped down to their racing garb, and one-by-one the announcer introduced them and called them to the starting line. My eager anticipation surprised me. I barely knew Robyn, but the romantic in me was hoping she would somehow pull off a great race—maybe even win. Of course, I reminded myself that, based on her attitude, the chances were slim. The starter raised his pistol, and I, along with the other Canadian supporters there that day, stood quietly awaiting the crack of the gun. An amoeba-like group of competitors ran the first stretch. Soon, the top Canadian, the top Australian, the top Brit and the top Kenyans started to break away from the pack. A few laps into the race, the serious contenders had put significant distance between themselves and the slower runners, who were now fading.

Robyn, not surprisingly, was not among the leaders. In fact, she was tied for last. My response, heartless as it may seem, was to laugh—*what the hell did you expect with a perspective like yours?* Hunkering down into my seat for what I now presumed was going to be a long, boring and uneventful race, I watched an insurmountable gap between the two groups of runners grow lap after lap. A 3,000-metre race is seven and a half laps of the track—it should take a good international female runner between eight and a half and nine minutes to complete. With four laps remaining, Robyn was easily 50 metres or more behind the lead group. As far as I was concerned, she was done—what was the point in continuing? I felt sorry for her, embarrassed that she was having such a poor showing. She should have never gone in this race, especially knowing that she was so unprepared.

Then, finally, with three laps to go and the entire stadium cheering on the leaders, Robyn passed someone. And she didn't stop there. She passed another runner and another runner and another. It was as if she had suddenly grown wings. Her move had been noticed—everyone in the stadium was now on their feet and cheering. Robyn continued to push until she found herself in fourth place. By now, Angela Chalmers, the top Canadian, was leading comfortably. A gold and bronze medal awaited Canada if Robyn could just pass one more runner and move into that third place. The crowd, now frantically cheering, tried desperately to encourage her into the bronze medal position. Completely caught up in the excitement, I too was on my feet screaming as loudly as I possibly could. When Robyn moved into third place, the entire stadium erupted. There was now less than 400 metres to go, and she was gunning for the silver medal. Going down the backstretch, she flew past the British runner and moved into second place.

As Angela crossed the finish line, easily taking the gold medal and setting a new Commonwealth Games record, everyone cheered and acknowledged her accomplishment. I watched as she turned around to see who was in second, clap her hands and then cover her mouth in surprise. The expression of shock on Angela's face confirmed that no one, not even her teammates, had expected Robyn to finish second. The two runners embraced and celebrated one another's efforts. While the remaining runners finished the race, Robyn and Angela began their victory lap with a Canadian flag flowing between them. It was a sports writer's dream and, not surprisingly, the moment would own the entire front page of the *Times Colonist* the next day.

I choked up. I was awed by an amazing display of the human spirit, a willingness to go so hard. I'd been expecting to watch Robyn get destroyed by her competitors. I hadn't believed that she could win the race with her attitude: "doing the best that she could." Everything that I had been taught, everything that I knew to be true, and everything that I believed regarding how a real competitor approached racing, had been challenged in those final minutes of the race. I had been certain that you couldn't have a perspective like Robyn's and perform like she had—it was impossible. But I had just seen it with my own eyes. Now I was curious. *How the hell had she done that?*

There was only one way to find out—ask for that second date.

That evening Fiona and I went down to Victoria's Inner Harbour to check out the free concert. Every night during the Commonwealth Games, bands performed to enormous crowds packed into the downtown streets. The Crash Test Dummies were performing that night. After the opening act was finished, the announcer walked onto the stage and brought Robyn and Angela with him. The crowd went crazy.

I took one look at Fiona and we both know what I had to do. "I'll see you back at the house later."

"Remember, play your cards patiently with Robyn!" yelled Fiona as I vanished into the cheering crowd.

The crowd, reluctant to let me through, slowed me down, so when I arrived Robyn was nowhere in sight. I waded out of the crowd toward what appeared to be the backstage entrance. Not surprisingly, there was a security guard standing there. *Go big or go home, Jase.*

"I'm here to see Robyn Meagher."

"Yeah. So?"

"Is there somebody you can call on your walkie-talkie? Someone backstage, maybe?"

He looked at me for a long while. I imagine he was thinking, *I either call someone or I stand here and listen to this guy all night.* He pulled out his walkie-talkie. "Is there anyone backstage?"

"Yeah, I'm here," answered an equally unenthused voice.

"Can you find some runner named Robyn and tell her that . . . what's your name?"

"Jason. Jason Dorland."

"Tell her that some guy named Jason is here at the gate waiting for her."

"Yeah, I'll tell her," the voice crackled back.

"There, that's all I can do."

Ten minutes passed. Then 20. Then 30. As the Crash Test Dummies played in the background, their lead singer's trademark baritone voice booming over the audience, my friend the security guard and I stood there not saying a word. Clearly he thought I just wasn't getting the hint. I was either too stupid or too stubborn, or some combination of both. But I'd waited this long and I didn't care how ridiculous I looked—I wasn't leaving.

Almost a full hour after the original message from my wingman, I saw Robyn come down the stairs off the stage and walk toward me and the exit. Or, was it the exit and me? I wasn't sure if she was just leaving or if she was actually coming out to see me. It didn't matter; I didn't care. If nothing else, my perseverance had sent her the message that I was really interested.

When she arrived at the gate, I shook her hand softly to say hello and to congratulate her on her efforts in the race earlier that day. She smiled and graciously accepted my well wishes. Leaning forward to rest, Robyn put both arms on the temporary gate. With the streetlights glistening in her eyes, she looked more beautiful than she had at the beach a week earlier.

My heart was pounding—I was nervous. No, I was really nervous. Sadly, however, Fiona's advice had now fallen hard to the ground beside me. I reached out and placed my hand on top of Robyn's—this was my idea of "going big." *Whoa there, cowboy—are you crazy? Didn't you hear what Fiona said? "Nice and easy!" You are so going to blow this.*

No sooner had I put my hand on hers than she stood up and pulled hers away. *Okay, big shooter, how can you salvage this one?*

I needed to do something quick. Even the guard had noticed and had now turned his back and was walking away slowly, probably doing everything he could not to laugh out loud.

I pretended that nothing awkward had just happened. "Do you have time for a walk? Or would you like to go get something to eat?"

"I really do need to get home and into bed," she politely answered. "I have the 1,500 metres on Wednesday, and I need to be rested for that." *Damn, I'm done!* "But why don't you give me a call sometime this week?" *But I'm not dead! Way to go, Jase!*

Accepting what I saw as a temporary defeat, I conceded. "Okay, that sounds good. If I don't talk to you before Wednesday, have a good race." I turned to walk away, then stopped and added, "Oh, and congratulations again on your race today. That was an incredible performance."

It was a warm and beautiful night. Meandering through some of the oldest neighbourhoods in Victoria, I could smell the sweet scent of barbecue lingering in the night air. People were still out on their porches soaking up the last precious moments of another perfect day. Everyone seemed to be in a good mood. Why shouldn't they be? Summertime was the reprieve that all West Coasters lived for. It was payback for the dreary winter months that we endured from November to March when rain, fog, wind and cold, damp air chilled you to the bone and sent you in search of a warm fire.

It had been quite a day for me. The race had been spectacular, but seeing Robyn again had certainly been a bonus, no matter how awkward our chance meeting had been. My head was spinning. Was Robyn interested in pursuing things a little further? She had said to call her, and I saw that as an invitation to see where things could go. I wasn't done yet, but I did need to listen to and heed Fiona's advice—take it slow!

Fiona was still up when I got back and eager to hear how things had gone. She put on some tea and sat me down. "Okay, I want to hear all the goods."

I took a deep breath, exhaled and, at the end of my exhale, I offered, "It went okay."

"Okay? That's it? Come on, there has to be more—what happened?" Fiona was persistent. "Why were you gone so long?"

"I had to wait a whole hour to see her. We had a quick chat. I told her how impressed I was with her race and that was about it."

"Oh. That's not too terribly exciting."

"Yeah, well. I asked her if she wanted to go for something to eat, but she was worried about her race later this week. That's fair enough. I would've said the same. So then she went straight home."

"Then why were you gone so long?"

"I told you, I waited for an hour until she finally came out to see me."

"Did she know you were there?"

"I'm not sure."

"Yikes, that's not great. How did you leave it?"

"She said to call her later this week."

Fiona jumped out of her chair, "Well that's good. Why are you so bummed? She asked you to call her. That's a good sign."

"Yeah, I guess. We'll just see what happens. I'm not holding my breath."

I was trying not to get too excited about how things might work out, but I'd be lying if I said I wasn't hanging on to the possibility that something could happen. Patience was going to be the ticket—something I had never possessed. I also tried to remind myself that, unlike me, Robyn was still a full-time athlete. I certainly knew how anal I could be around race time. This was her competitive time of the year and I needed to cut her some slack.

Arriving home in Vancouver and sharing the details of my trip with Pat and Trev was a little different. They had seen the race on TV. They knew how that had turned out; what they wanted know was whether I'd seen Robyn again. In typical male fashion, I told them that I had and that she had told me to give her a call. They both responded with high-fives. There was no way in hell I was sharing the part about waiting for an hour and how much of a loser I had been when I tried to hold her hand—that was staying with me.

The following week Pat, Trev and I sat down to watch Robyn's race on TV. It looked as though she was having a decent race, right up until the last corner when another runner "bumped" her as they jockeyed for position. She ended up finishing seventh. I could appreciate that running was supposed to be a non-contact sport, but how Robyn had managed not to "bump" the same competitor back was beyond me. I was of the mind that if someone was going to interrupt my ability to win, then retaliation was in order.

Showing great restraint, I waited an entire two days before calling. My strategy was to seem interested but not desperate. I was triumphant—the second date was on. The plan was simple—return to Victoria, meet for a walk and then dinner back at Fiona's place— without Fiona. The way I saw it, the walk was crucial, primarily because Ike could then work his magic. If he was going to assist me in my quest for Robyn, then he would need to be involved in as many of our dates as possible. Shallow? Perhaps. But I was determined to have Robyn—to win her. And, as I had done with everything that I had won in my life, I was prepared to do whatever it took.

It worked. We returned to Fiona's from our walk with Robyn holding Ike's leash. For dinner, I prepared a dish guaranteed to impress: baked sea bass in an orange marinade with dill served over a bed of fragrant basmati rice and steamed asparagus decoratively arranged on the plate. It was wicked. For dessert, we had peanut butter and chocolate pie in a graham cracker crust with a bit of soy ice cream. Robyn enjoyed every bite. Man, she could pack it away. I loved a woman who wasn't afraid to eat. There was no picking at her meal or leaving a small symbolic bite on the plate to say that she was in control of her appetite.

After dinner we made some tea and moved into the living room. We talked about family and then ventured into future plans around school and running. Sitting next to Robyn, contemplating a potentially romantic evening, any normal guy would have been thinking about his next move. Not me—I was thinking about her next race.

"Robyn, that was a good race you had a few weeks ago, but at one point you were losing badly. And then all of the sudden, you just took off. It was like you snapped. What happened out there? What did you say to yourself? How did you do that?"

I was convinced that what would follow would revolutionize the way elite athletes competed in the future. Unfortunately, what Robyn offered up was anything but.

"Well, I knew going into the race that I didn't have the fitness that the other competitors did. I decided that I was going to pace myself to the halfway point and then see how I was feeling. When I got to lap four—halfway—I felt pretty good. I started to push. As I began to run faster, I started to pass some of the other runners. When I did that, the crowd cheered. As they cheered, this energy came out of the stands and onto the track. I was able to suck up that energy and, somehow, it gave me the speed I needed to run even faster. The faster I ran, the more they cheered and the more energy they gave me. In the end, it was really the crowd that enabled me to run as fast as I did."

'Scuse me? Before I had asked my question, I thought I had entertained the most plausible and probable answers that Robyn could muster given how "non-competitive" she was. More importantly, they were answers that I could have partially swallowed and still been interested in dating her. But when I heard the load of pathetic, feel-good, Girl Guide bullshit come ever so softly out of her lips, I couldn't believe my ears. I was speechless. It was quite honestly the most ridiculous thing I had ever heard—an athlete relating their racing experience to energy from the crowd. How she was not too embarrassed to share that with me, I had no idea. Even if I, in a moment of complete and utter weakness, had entertained the idea that a cheering crowd could somehow replace my inner belief that I had to kill someone to win, I would never have been stupid enough to share it with someone. Plus, I didn't buy one bit of her crazy explanation.

In an attempt to keep our conversation going, I mustered, "Really?" After a long, long pause I figured it was time to share my theory about how she did it.

"I was thinking it was more like, you know, you were running along and you happened to look around and see that you were almost in last place. And the thought of that made you angry. And you got madder and madder until you began to hate everyone else on that track. You hated them so much that you wanted to kill them. And then you snapped and took off. You started running faster and faster, passing each of your competitors one after the next. Until you had only one person left to catch—Angela. And if you had gotten angrier sooner, I bet you would have caught her, too. In the end, wasn't it your hatred of the other runners that inspired you to do what you did?"

The look on Robyn's face said it perfectly: *Are you for real?* But to my amazement, she wanted to continue the discussion. She smiled and said, "Not quite. In fact, I've had coaches who have encouraged me to not be so friendly with my competitors before a race, and I tried it. Invariably I don't race any better and I feel totally exhausted at the end of the race."

"Okay, so if you don't use hatred to motivate yourself—the only tactic I've ever known—then what do you use? What do you say to yourself before a race, Robyn? How do you psych yourself up?"

Hoping—no, praying—the question would lead our conversation back to some form of normalcy, I waited for her to respond. If, in a million years, I had known what her answer would be, I would never have asked the question. Robyn was about to ruin the entire night. She paused, took a breath and offered this one up: "Well, I approach each race like a personal journey."

That's it. I'm done. Any more of this New Age crap and I'm out of here.

"Before each race," she continued, "before I step onto the track, I hold for myself the highest intention that at some point during this race I will learn something about myself that will not only make me a better runner, but a better person as well." She paused. "That's it. I try to stay calm, focused and intent on finding my best performance on the day. Simple."

No, you're right, that is simple—simply a waste of my time.

This conversation was becoming ridiculous and annoying. Robyn's approach offended me. If she had been a weekend jogger and entered the odd 10K race, no problem—I'm good with that sort of approach. But she wasn't. She was a national team carded athlete, which meant that she received money from the Canadian government every month to assist her in her pursuit of winning medals—gold ones. If she thought this sort of Oprah-styled, self-help garbage was going to help her win races, she was seriously mistaken.

No matter how beautiful Robyn was, how intriguing, how mysterious, I couldn't stomach her anymore. She had obviously been misled by some wussy-ass coach or some New Age flavour-of-the-month book and I began thinking that it was my job to set the poor child straight. Not knowing exactly what to say, I made my way to the kitchen to get some more tea and gather my thoughts. When I returned, Robyn offered me the perfect opportunity to declare my disapproval and straighten her out about a few things.

"How about you, Jason? How did you race? How did you get yourself mentally prepared for racing?"

"Okay, when I used to race, Robyn, I would sit in my seat in the starting gates and look across at all of the other competitors—

the guy in my seat in every other boat. And in my head I would say, 'Buddy, if you think you're going to win, you're crazy. Because I'm prepared to do whatever it takes to ensure I win and you lose.'" Robyn's soft, welcoming smile was slowly sliding off her face. That encouraged me to continue. "In fact, if the rules had permitted, I would have been willing to take my oar out of my oarlock and bash anyone over the head if that would have helped me win."

Kaboom! Feeling quite proud of myself, I sat waiting for her reply. *Okay, Oprah, whatcha got now?*

Much to my disappointment, Robyn offered nothing—she was silent. I saw it as her admission of defeat—there was no way she could come back from that. I had sunk her airy-fairy philosophy. Gloating over and relishing the painful moments of our awkward silence, I waited.

Finally she said, "Well, Jason, I'm sorry you feel that way."

The next morning, over breakfast, Fiona was eager to hear how her happy couple was doing. Any progress? First kiss? All that sort of stuff. When I shared the details of the evening—the meal, the dinner conversation, moving into the living room—Fiona was encouraged. When I told her about my questions and Robyn's answers, and how that had led to my zinger of a comeback, she just looked blankly at me and said, "What? You said what? You've gotta be kidding, Jason!"

She clearly wasn't as amused as I was.

"Robyn wouldn't appreciate that. What were you thinking? She's different from the other athletes you know, Jason. 'Bash someone over the head with your oar?' Oh my, that wasn't good." After a few more bites of toast, Fiona asked, "How did you leave it?"

"We didn't really leave it any particular way. She just sort of left."

"Oh boy."

On the return ferry later that day, I sat quietly tuning in and out of the conversations that surrounded me on the packed viewing deck. Eventually losing myself in the picturesque scenery provided by the Gulf Islands, I began reflecting on my date with Robyn.

What a jackass! My comment about the oar had been ridiculous. Even if I did believe that, and I did, what kind of nutbar says that to a woman on a date—especially someone like Robyn? I knew she was going to react the way she did. Why did I find it so compelling, so satisfying, to climb up the nose of a soft-spoken person like her? I couldn't imagine too many people would enjoy, let alone tolerate, being around that sort of blatant aggression. Such deliberate arrogance, tempting some poor soul to bite, to challenge me and then choke as they realize too late what they've taken on. And then, finally, in some perverse way, taking pleasure in making someone squirm with my archaic, macho bullshit approach to competition.

How had I gotten so bitter—so mad at the world? Where along the way had I become such a jerk? These questions hit me hard, and I figured I had better find the answers soon, or the rest of my life was going to be very lonely.

The next morning Ike and I woke up early and took off down the street to the Endowment Lands—miles of idyllic wooded trails—our usual running spot. I had a marathon to get ready for and not much time to prepare—it was time to crank up the mileage. After realizing what a miserable jerk I had become, I knew I had lots to process, but I figured it was nothing that a few hours of getting lost in those beautiful evergreens couldn't fix.

I started to think—hard. It had been six years since Seoul, and although the rowing nightmares still showed up, they were nowhere near as frequent. As for my eating, things were better, but I still struggled with it at times. I realized I had made progress, but there was still an edge around the loss. That edge was a wall that kept everyone at bay.

Robyn was a perfect example. She was everything I could have hoped for in a woman, and even though our evening had ended in disaster, I was still interested. She intrigued me. The fact that she didn't roll over and play polite was something I hadn't experienced much of before. I wanted another chance to see her, but given how things had gone, I wasn't sure how to proceed.

As soon as I got home, I phoned Fiona. "What do you think the chances are of my seeing her again?" I asked sheepishly.

Her tone was sarcastic. "Well, given the wonderful impression you made the other night, I'm sure Robyn is pining for your call as we speak."

"That bad, eh?"

"Yeah, I'd say so. I'm seeing her later this week. I'll suss things out."

Fiona did speak to Robyn, and I learned just what a forgiving soul Robyn was. Our third date was another walk with Ike beside us. My strategy for getting back into Robyn's good books was keeping the conversation light—no talk of sports or competition in any form whatsoever.

At the end of our walk, I handed her an invitation to my birthday party. It was the beginning of August and my 30th birthday was in a few weeks. I had made an invitation to the party that revealed some of the goals I had set for myself when I was 18, things that I wanted to have accomplished or have in my life by the time my third decade ended. The first and second were being married and having four children. The third was being a millionaire. Oh, the things we imagine when we're young.

She laughed at the sentiment on the invitation and appreciated the gesture, but she was off to India, London and possibly New York for some races. I wished her a safe trip and good racing overseas. Just before I got in the car, I asked her if I could call her when she got back in September. She said yes, and I was alive for another day.

6 ━━━━━━━

WINNING PROPOSITIONS

Halfway into September, ever the control freak, I was going crazy. I couldn't play the "be patient" game any longer. I called Fiona.

"What do you think of this? What if I fly down to New York and surprise Robyn at the New York City Mile—what do you think? Good idea?" Silence. Then, more silence. "What do you think?" I said with a little more insistence. "Is that a good idea or what?"

"Well, she'll certainly get the message that you're interested," was Fiona's response. "Why don't you wait until she gets back and then just come over here? You can stay with me and then you guys can go on a few dates. You know, take it slow—like I've been telling you? Remember, Jase—she's still competing. You're done with that part of your life, but she's not. You need to remember what that life was like for you and appreciate how Robyn still spends her days."

Even though I realized that Fiona was kiboshing my idea, her words went in one ear and right out the other. As I had done all my life if I didn't like someone's response, I moved on to the next sounding board to get the answer I was looking for. I ran the idea by Pat and Trev, thinking of course that, being guys, they would get it.

Trev was excited. "Great idea, Jase. She'll be blown away by that. Go for it!" He thought that because guys didn't do stuff like that anymore, Robyn would think it was romantic. Pat, on the other hand, was cautiously supportive. Naturally I liked Trev's response better.

The next minute I was on the phone looking into flights. Sure, financially I was living the life of a student and there was no way I could afford it, but I didn't care. I figured "go big or go home." I returned to the best-case/worst-case scenario that was by now becoming my playbook for this "relationship" and realized that I could, once again, live with the worst case. I figured a weekend in New York on my own was the worst case—not bad in my books. I called Fiona again. She convinced me to at least call Robyn and let her know I was coming.

Robyn was at her parents' place in Mulgrave, Nova Scotia, but I only knew their names and where they lived. A quick 411 call and I was set. I dialled the number and waited.

With each ring, my butterflies grew larger. I had heard all about Robyn's folks and family during our talks. I knew that her mom was tiny and soft-spoken, and that her dad was a big guy who continued to spend his time at the local docks where he worked as a longshoreman. My stereotypical image of him inspired me to hope that her mom answered the phone.

After a few more rings, I got my wish. Robyn's mom was indeed quiet, but also polite and not at all put off by the notion that a complete stranger was phoning looking for her daughter.

"She's not here right at the moment. Can I tell her who called?"

As politely as I could, without sounding like Eddie Haskell from *Leave It to Beaver*, I spoke up. "My name is Jason Dorland. I'm a friend of Robyn's. I was just hoping to catch up with her." That was fair, and true.

"Well, she's at her sister's in Antigonish. Would you like the number there?" *Would I ever!*

"Hi, Robyn. It's Jason," was all I said when Robyn came to the phone.

"Oh. Hi, Jason." Silence. Dead silence. I wished I could see her face. I desperately wanted to know how this was playing out in Antigonish. I started to panic. "How was India? How did your racing go in London? Are you enjoying your time with your family?"

I figured a quick barrage of questions would buy me the required time to plan my big question—the reason for the call. I knew Robyn was answering them because I could hear her voice coming through on the phone—I just wasn't paying attention to her words. When there was a slight pause I asked, "How would you feel if I flew down to New York and watched you race this weekend?"

There was a long silence. "Umm" was the first sound that came squeaking over the phone line. It wouldn't have been my first choice of things I wanted to hear, but at least she hadn't hung up.

Robyn struggled through all the reasons it would not be good for me to come to New York. We chatted a little longer and then she said, "Thanks for calling." I had just been shot down—again.

With any other woman, I would only have had to smell a hint of disinterest and I'd be walking the other way. But Robyn wasn't any other woman. For her I was willing to endure pain, humiliation and suffering. We met a few more times during the fall that year. More walks with Ike along beaches and trails. Things weren't progressing at a rate even close to what other people might consider encouraging. Just before I left for Christmas in Ontario, I built up the courage to ask Robyn if there was any chance of us becoming more than just friends. Her answer was no. She said that she enjoyed our walks and visits, but that at this time in her life she just wanted to focus on her running and keep things as they were, simply remain friends.

I replied, "I have enough girl friends to rock the Queen Mary." She laughed, but the point was made. I was interested in moving this along and she wasn't. Our timing was off.

I gave her a CD. It included a new Larry Gowan song, "When There's Time for Love." I knew it was a sappy thing to do, but to me it explained everything perfectly. The song appeared to be written just for us:

> *The timing's wrong*
> *You're out there eager to fly*
> *I'll say so long*
> *But I'll sure be watching the sky*
> *When your wheels finally touch the ground*
> *Look me up, I'll be around.*

Ike, school and training for another Knee Knacker provided me with enough to occupy my time. It was late February on the West Coast—early spring for Vancouver—the cherry blossoms were out and the worst of the rain was over. Life was good. I was slowly recovering from the disappointment of not winning Robyn's approval. As much as I really wanted it to work out, I had conceded defeat and, with Fiona's advice, started dating other women.

My health was improving too. Even though I was still running lots of miles every week in preparation for my annual 50-kilometre race along the Baden-Powell Trail, I was eating much more. Gaining weight made me look differently at my running. When I had rowed in Seoul, I hovered around 188 pounds. Since then I had grown half an inch and had a bigger frame. I figured if I started weight lifting again I could reach 200 pounds or even a little more—a weight I had easily maintained while training at Shawnigan.

In some running and triathlon events, there is a weight category known as Clydesdale, named aptly for those beautiful and powerful horses that don't possess the speed of a quarter horse but can work all day. That's how I saw myself as a runner—not much speed to speak of, but once I got my big legs moving they kept going for a long time. Even though the Knee Knacker didn't have that specific category, I was going to create it for myself. If I could start the race at or above 200 pounds, then maybe my performance would improve because I would have more reserves and better core strength. The bonus would be that my appearance would change for the better. Most importantly, as usual, it provided a new challenge, something to chase once again.

In March, Pat, Trev and I got a notice from our landlord saying that he was selling the house, our beloved home. Trev decided to move to Victoria and live with his girlfriend. Pat moved in with some other medical students. Things for Ike and me were a little more challenging. When you have a dog and you live in a major city, you have a harder time finding a landlord who will accept you as a tenant. I put up notices and spread the word that we were looking, but as soon as the question of Ike came up it was always the same answer—no pets. How do you tell someone that your dog is not like other dogs? That he doesn't dig, chew, smell or crap all over the floor? You don't. You can't.

Luckily an old friend, Wendy Mitchell, offered to let us stay with her until we found something suitable. Wendy was also from a Ridley family, and her husband, Mike, was a wisecracking, cocky young guy with a big heart and generous nature. They lived in Coquitlam, a suburb of Vancouver, and they too had a dog. Maddy was an adorable high-energy black Lab cross. Ike and Maddy became good buds and I settled into living in our new home quite nicely.

Amid renovations, busy schedules and the hectic life of going to school and trying to get in enough training runs, we had a blast living there. The one-month offer stretched into two, then three, and so on. Every chance he got, Mike introduced me as the nightmare that came for one month and stayed for seven. During that time, naturally, the topic of women came up. There was nothing that Mike enjoyed more than analyzing my love life. When we chatted about Robyn, he would say I was crazy to hang on to a pipe dream.

He, like Fiona, said I should get out there and play. Wendy stayed out of it. If she had an opinion, she wouldn't share it. Ever kind and supportive, she would just laugh and tell Mike to be nice.

While living with Wendy and Mike, I joined a local Toastmasters International group. I was coming into my final year at Emily Carr and I was required to present my thesis project in front of a panel and accompanying audience. Standing up in front of a crowd made my chest tighten like a vise, so I needed to develop my public-speaking skills. After a few meetings, you are encouraged to perform an icebreaker, a talk about the one thing you're supposed to know more about than anything else in your life—yourself. My instructions were to share something significant about my life. Up until that point, my life had been rowing—to write about anything else would have seemed fabricated.

In the week leading up to the talk, I hemmed and hawed about whether or not to divulge the absolute truth. I wasn't worried so much about whether or not they could handle it, but rather if I could. Eventually I decided I was simply going to write down all of the things I should have said in the year following Seoul and see what came out. To my surprise, what showed up was softer than I had expected. The bitterness and anger that had once owned my voice when I spoke of the Olympics had changed ever so slightly. My language wasn't as venomous as it had once been.

I was surprised—and pleasantly. What had changed? More importantly, what had changed it? Had I just simply grown up? Was it that almost seven years had gone by since the race? Or, had seeing Robyn's race and subsequently talking about her approach to competition had more of an impact on me than I was willing to acknowledge? Maybe—I wasn't sure. Maybe it was a combination of all three. One thing was certain, I had turned a corner—I was beginning to see things differently. Unbeknownst to me, I had been healing. I was still healing. I was coming out of the darkest place I had ever been in my life.

On the day of the icebreaker, and with only hours to go until I was supposed to get up and share my story, I was struggling with the ending. While hurriedly searching and punching on an old computer in the basement, I heard someone come in upstairs. It was my good friend Karyn Mitchell, Mike's sister. She had dropped by to see who was home.

She came downstairs and asked, "So, Jase, are you ready for your big speech tonight?"

"Not quite. I'm not sure if I've nailed the ending or not." I paused for a moment. "Would you mind if I read you what I have so far?" I sounded like a terrified little boy.

"Not at all. I'd love to hear it." She sat down beside me and waited.

With a deep breath, I began.

Have you ever had a dream? I mean a real-life dream? One that controlled every aspect of your daily life? Where nothing was more important than your dream? Where your health, your friends, your family—everything—took a back seat to your all-consuming dream? Not one where you say to yourself, "Yeah, that would be kind of nice." But one where you say, "I would do anything and give anything to have that come true."

I had a dream like that. It started as an innocent fantasy when I was eight years old. By the time I was 18, it had grown into what some might call an obsession. And for the next six years it would influence where I went to university, my social life and ultimately who I am today.

In the early afternoon of the 25th of September 1988, in Seoul, Korea, I had my one shot at realizing my lifelong dream. It was the Olympic final of the men's eight in rowing, and I was sitting three seats from the bow, in lane six, wearing a Canadian singlet. Canada had won the gold medal in Los Angeles in 1984 and that made us defending Olympic champions. Although we had four members of that crew in our boat, we were not the same crew. We were bigger, stronger and faster. During the two races leading up to the final, we had shown tremendous speed in certain sections of the race. It was our chance to put those two races together and have the race of our lives. Going into the final, the Australian coach had said, "If the Canadians are anywhere in contention with 500 metres to go, the race will be over."

Less than six minutes after the starter's command, we crossed the line in sixth place. Far from what we had expected of ourselves, and perhaps farther from what others had expected of us. My emotions ranged from anger to disbelief to nothing. My senses were completely numb. Years of sacrifice—physically, financially and emotionally— all for what? That was it; my one shot was gone. I would never have that chance again. That Olympic gold medal was everything to me. As I saw it, it was the only reason for going to Seoul. Getting to the Olympics was not the dream; it was merely part of the process. To go to the Olympics and not come home with that medal meant failure. It meant that all those years of training were for naught. Going to the Olympics was not about representing my country or competing with the best in the world; it was about medals. And the one that mattered most was gold.

When I returned home, I found the *Globe and Mail* from September 25th. On the cover of the sports page was a picture of our eight slumped over our oars after the finish of the race. The headline read, "Canadians Bomb Out in Seoul."

My family and I never talked about the race. They simply said they were proud of me regardless of the outcome and we left it at that. I didn't phone anyone when I got home. I didn't want to see anyone. I didn't want to talk to anyone. I just wanted to hide. When I did run into people, it was always the same thing, "What happened?" And that just brought it all back. So I figured the best thing to do was to go somewhere where nobody knew me. I chose Australia. After five months in Melbourne and one month travelling the East Coast, I felt I was ready to come home. My plan was to return to Vancouver Island and resume my training for 1992. I wasn't ready to give up on my dream just yet.

I began training in September of 1989. At first it was going well. I felt my strength and endurance returning with each workout. However, with those improvements came flashbacks of the race in Seoul, and those flashbacks were beginning to wear thin on my emotions. Initially I had used the loss in Seoul as a form of motivation. It was vindication I was after. I saw my next Olympic race purely as revenge. As I found out, revenge is a powerful motivating force, but the effect is short-lived. With revenge comes an enormous amount of hatred and anger. Maintaining those emotions was making me an extremely miserable young man.

It had become too much. I began questioning my reasons for wanting to go to the Olympics a second time. What if I lost again? Train four more years for 1996? Then 2000? When would it end? I was not about to find out. Six months into my training I decided that I had had enough. If I continued at this rate, I wasn't going to make it to 1992, not physically and especially not emotionally. I phoned my coach and told him. He said he understood. We reminisced about old times for a few minutes. I hung up, had good cry and said to myself, "That's it. It's over. Never again."

Was it over, though? Was it truly out of my life? Sure, I could say the actual physical hands-on side of rowing was gone, but what about the mental side? All those emotions left over from Seoul? What about them?

Since that day there have been more talks and more tears, and along with them a growing realization of what the Olympics now mean to me. The feelings from the race will always be there. The disappointment. The pain. The frustration. The "what ifs?" What if things had been different? What if we had won? How would that have changed my life? Would that have affected the person I am today? Lots of questions, but no answers. There will never be answers. But what there will be is a stronger belief in, "Yes, I went to the Olympics and I didn't win a gold medal." But maybe I truly am a better person for it.

Crack! Right there. That was it. That was as far as I was getting. Damn! I had almost made it, too. I choked and stopped. Tears started to well up in my eyes and then stream down my cheeks.

Karyn sat quietly. Then she reached out her hand and took mine, squeezing it gently. "It's okay, Jase. Take your time." After a few moments, I was able to breathe normally and continue.

Perhaps it was a test that I will continue to learn, strengthen and grow from until one day I can return that knowledge and strength to someone else.

In looking back, I don't regret having gone to the Olympics. It was a dream. It was my dream. And I gave to that dream everything I had.

I squeezed Karyn's hand, seeking out her added strength to keep my emotions in check for just a little longer. Another short pause and I was off again.

Sure, falling short hurt like hell. But that's life. Sometimes things work out the way we want. And sometimes they don't. But that doesn't mean we shouldn't all have dreams. I still have dreams. I dream of someday being a great husband and dad; I dream of being a teacher who makes a tremendous difference in a child's life. And I'll go after those dreams the same way that I went after my Olympic dream. And if they come true . . . great. And if they don't, well, I'll have more dreams. Because when we stop dreaming, we stop living.

With my hand now sweating in Karyn's, I was feeling more embarrassed than anything. Naturally, I was beginning to wonder if this whole icebreaker thing was a good idea. Karyn was one person, and a good friend at that, but I was going to have to tell this story to a room full of complete strangers?

Karyn stood up and gestured for me to do the same. She put her arms around me and said, "That was beautiful, Jase. That really was." Her hug made me feel, for the first time in my life, that it was safe to say that what happened in Seoul had messed me up more than I had ever been willing to admit to anyone, perhaps even myself.

Rushing out the door, I left a copy of my speech on the kitchen counter for Mike and Wendy to read when they got home. I jumped in my car and sped off to the community hall that hosted our club. The entire way, I tried to convince myself that it was a good idea and that turning back would be a chicken-shit thing to do.

Just before the end of the first half of the meeting, I was called to the front of the room to give my speech. I was wearing my heart-rate monitor under my shirt, and when I looked down

I saw that I was doing the equivalent of a recovery run, I knew I had some work to do on relaxing. My dad had been an award-winning Toastmaster when he was younger; however, if that gene was in me, it would take some serious mining to uncover it.

I stood up and walked to the lectern. I looked out at all of the people smiling politely as the membership book encourages them to do. I took a deep breath. I shared my story without faltering once. The encouraging applause was soothing. As it was with Karyn, I knew they had heard me. Some of them with tears in their eyes. I felt good. I had finally kicked open a door that had been tightly locked for years. I was now eager to throw away the whipping stick I had been carrying.

When I got home, my beautiful boy Ike was there, wagging his tail and dancing around me, happy as always to see me again. Then Maddy greeted me. Then Mike called out from the bedroom, "Jason, get the hell in here!" I knew by his brash but playful tone that I was in for an earful of sarcastic shots.

He and Wendy were in bed reading when I walked in. "What the hell is this?" Mike asked, holding up my speech. "How did you get up and read this tonight? Wendy and I were both blubber-blubber-blubber trying to get through your speech." Wendy was laughing beside him making sure that he didn't go too far. She knew more about my Olympic experience than Mike did and had always been careful when discussing it. "This is beautiful, Jason." Coming from Mike—that was saying something. He didn't blow sunshine unless he wanted to.

I was now laughing with them, thinking back to a few hours prior when I was standing before my Toastmasters club completely exposed and being okay with that. "I don't know. I just got up and read it. It was okay. It felt good to do that."

"I guess so. Man, this is something else," said Mike, still playfully laughing and wanting to squeeze as much mileage out of this as he could.

Wendy finally spoke up. "What did everyone say afterwards?"

"Well, everyone was supportive. I mean, what are they going to say, right? But for the most part, their feedback was good. One of the things everyone does after a speech is jot down a few comments. I have them here but haven't had a chance to read them all. From what I've glanced at, however, people wrote some really nice things. It was a good night."

"Well, get them out and let's have a look." Mike gestured for me to pass them to him.

"Mike! They're Jason's comments and they might be personal," Wendy stepped in.

"Personal? He doesn't care."

"It's okay, Wen." I got them out and gave them to Mike.

"Well, I'm starving. I didn't eat much before I left. I didn't want to hurl 2,000 calories worth of food onto the poor souls in the front row. I'm going to get something to eat."

As I started to walk out of the room, Mike not looking up from reading the comments, spoke up again, "Oh, by the way, stalker boy, there's a message on the machine from the soft talker in Victoria."

"Get out!"

"I'm serious. Go have a listen. And either she needs a new phone or she needs to learn which end you speak into—Christ, I could hardly hear her." Mike cackled his usual laugh as I ran out to the kitchen to hear the message.

I hit the PLAY button. Sure enough, it was Robyn. Mike wasn't bullshitting. And, like he had warned, I could hardly hear her. I played it again trying to decipher her message. She was phoning to see how I was doing and if I was going to be in Victoria in the near future. *Yes!*

Over the next few months, Robyn and I met for a few dates in both Victoria and Vancouver. I finally followed Fiona's advice and took things slowly. After tearing a hamstring during a training session, Robyn had a lot more free time, and with no competitive meets in her immediate future, we were able to spend a fair amount of time together. With Ike always included in our plans, we went on hikes, walks or runs along our favourite trails. Given that I was still in school and Robyn was living on National Team Athletic Assistance, our "dates" were generally quite simple. Instead of going out on the town, we would get together and talk. We got to know each other. The more I learned about her—the more I liked her. She was smart, funny, thoughtful and not afraid to challenge my beliefs.

In late June she invited me to meet her sister, Erin, and brother-in-law, Kuz, short for Kuzumi, who lived in Abbotsford, a small farming community east of Vancouver. Knowing, or at least wanting to believe, that meeting her sister meant I was finally making some inroads, I was determined not to screw up the visit. Of course, Ike was invited too, and I bathed and brushed him until his trademark golden retriever feathers flowed behind him.

Thankfully, the interrogation I had expected during the visit never materialized. Instead it was easy conversation centred around family, gardens, pets and Robyn—surprisingly enough. Erin dished out some entertaining dirt on Robyn. It was harmless teasing, but it showed evidence of a family that had grown up not afraid to laugh at each other and themselves—nice.

By now, Robyn and I were becoming good friends, and I was okay with that. I enjoyed our visits and our phone conversations—we had great chats about all kinds of things. Even our discussions about sports were good. I had mellowed a little. I would even go so far as to say that a bit of Robyn's philosophy was beginning to rub off on me.

Up until then, I had approached each year's North Shore Knee Knacker race focused on beating my competitors. Even though I had no illusions of winning, once I got into the thick of it, I would assign countries to the runners who were either in front of me or behind me and proceed to do battle. I loved training for the races; spending hours and hours on the beautiful Baden-Powell trails with Ike and the others in our training group, but the way I approached competition wasn't quite working for me anymore. In the end I never enjoyed the races; they were seven-plus hours of trying to kill other runners—where was the fun in that?

I had kept my challenge of maintaining my weight at or above 200 pounds and put in some really good long training sessions in the weeks leading up to the race. Now, as I began my taper, my training runs felt relaxed and easy. I was sleeping well, and my resting heart rate each morning was around 36 or 37 beats per minute—I was fit and ready. The day of the race, I didn't use my default approach to competing—I just showed up and ran. I stayed focused on running a smart race and not only did I enjoy myself, but I broke seven hours. It was the most fun I had ever had racing.

Later that summer, one of Robyn's other five sisters, Shannon, and her husband and family drove from her farm in Saskatchewan to visit with Erin and Kuz. The sparks really flew during that visit. Not between Robyn and me, but between the sisters. Shannon and Erin took the opportunity to dish more dirt on their younger sister. It was a fun evening filled with delicious food, good conversation and some lively, spirited banter.

During dinner the siblings decided they would head to the beaches in White Rock the next day, and I was invited to come along. After enjoying a swim in the ocean and some extremely greasy fish and chips from a local vendor, we capped off another great day with a sunset stroll along the boardwalk in front of some beautiful cottage-style homes. I must have been on a roll because, after the walk, I was invited back to Erin and Kuz's to continue the day's visit. Erin whipped up more food and we all gathered around the dining room table and continued to chat, as I was sure they had done many times back home in Nova Scotia. The stories about Robyn kept coming one after the next. She was being a good sport about it all. She tried to defend herself from time to time, but each attempt was drowned out by laughter. They were good people and easy to be around.

With all of the food gone and the playful banter exhausted, the others excused themselves from the table and made their way to bed leaving Robyn and me alone. Up until this point we hadn't been alone together and there had never been a moment where I had felt the urge to assess the situation. However, that night, my radar was in overdrive, and I was desperately trying to sort out what all of the family time with me included meant.

Our conversation continued quite easily; we laughed as we revisited the events of the past few days. At some point, I felt Robyn relax, almost in a wave. That had never happened before. Not surprisingly, my inner voice started to chatter.

Jase, man. I know the rules you've been playing by and I admire you for staying true to those for this long, but my sense is the game just changed. The tides are turning, Big Boy. I think you should risk showing some initiative of the physical kind.

I wasn't so sure. The last time I'd tried that, I had been shot down—rather abruptly. The weekend had been such a good one; why screw it up now? Not initiating anything kept things safe. I avoided rejection, and I was more than okay with that.

You candy ass! You gotta be kidding. You're going to sit there and do nothing? So, that's it—you'll be Robyn's "friend" forever? That's embarrassing! Reach out and take hold of her hand—it's not like she's going to hit you.

Based on the stories that I had heard over the past two days, I wasn't too sure of that. I was guessing that Robyn was indeed capable of knocking me flat on my backside.

Look, just try it. Trust me on this; that last time was over a year ago. Come on, where did the go-big-or-go-home guy I used to know disappear to? Just do it and stop being such a wuss!

Well, I did have to agree, Robyn was different from the last time I had tried to hold her hand. We were different—we had become friends. What was the harm in trying, right? With my mind made up, I reached out and took her hand in mine and waited for her response—she smiled.

The game was over. When I had first met Robyn, yes, I was intrigued by the mystique of this beautiful, soft-spoken redhead. Her confidence, her knowledge and her approach to living were all so different from anyone I had met before. But now—I was attracted to how she challenged me to think differently about all sorts of things in my life—how she made me feel when I was around her. It was no longer about winning her—about having my trophy girlfriend. I had moved beyond that. I had genuinely fallen in like with Robyn the person—that was something I had never done before.

In September 1995, I began my last year at Emily Carr. Much to Mike and Wendy's relief I'm sure, Ike and I had finally moved out. Pat, Karyn and I had found a perfect house with a big fenced yard in the back for Ike.

My weekdays consisted of a brisk 30-minute morning walk with Ike to school, a day of classes and then a return trip. For our thesis project, we were required to come up with a topic that focused on one or more aspects of design in our chosen area of study and to apply that to a real-world project and present our final work to a panel of professional designers along with our peers, parents and instructors.

Being a huge fan of peanut butter and having just purchased a heavy-duty juicer that could also grind nuts and make delicious fresh creamy nut butters, I became obsessed with making my own peanut butter. One day, perusing the isles of the local bulk food store, I thought it might be interesting to throw some other ingredients into the grinder, like different nuts and seeds, dark chocolate chips and coffee beans, butterscotch chips and pecans, dark chocolate and M&Ms; I even threw Skor bars into the mix.

It was a no-brainer. When you mix those sorts of ingredients together you get a concoction that is as close to culinary perfection as you could well imagine. These delicious spreads went with anything and everything—toast, pancakes, crackers, ice cream, fingers. I started making them for friends and family as gifts. The response wasn't just "thank you," it was "any chance I could get some more?" They were a hit, and I thought I had something resembling a design project.

I took the idea to one of my instructors who was quick to remind me that this was not a business school and that designing the packaging was the objective, not starting a viable business. Fair enough, I thought, but I wasn't going to spend an entire year on something and only have a letter grade to show for it. What I wanted was something more than a school project.

I took to the trails with Ike for some serious brainstorming about the name brand for my peanut butters. After numerous runs, it struck me one afternoon that all this time I had been running with the name—Ike! These were fun and playful peanut butters and what was more fun and playful than a golden retriever? Nothing, as far as I was concerned. The best part was that if this thing took off, Ike would forever be immortalized on a food label—what better way to keep him around?

The next day I ran the name by one of my instructors.

"This food is for humans, correct?" she asked.

"Yes, of course it is."

"Well then, don't put a dog on it. People won't buy food for humans with a dog on the label."

"Okay. I'll go on there with him," I replied. "But he's staying. He represents exactly what the products are all about—fun, playful and extraordinary. Besides, he's a beautiful golden retriever and people love golden retrievers."

She looked at me straight in the eye and said, "Jason, I like my dog, too. But come on."

I didn't know what to say to that. I had taken her remarks personally. So I said nothing and after a long uncomfortable pause, I got up and left the meeting. I was bound and determined to show my instructor, and anyone else who questioned the validity of having Ike on the label, that he was the perfect poster boy for my human food—despite being furry and having a knack for rolling in shit.

While I was walking home with Ike that afternoon, the remainder of the name came to me—Skeet & Ike's Not Just Nuts Spreads. For me, it was logical—the label would have a person on it and the name showed the spreads had other ingredients than nuts. Along with being a clever play on words, all that mattered was that Ike was going to be on a food label come hell or high water. I didn't care if they failed me—deep down in my gut, I knew my approach was the right one.

As school came to an end that spring, my Skeet & Ike's packaging project had come together nicely and I was about as ready to present as I was going to be. I had also found my business partner, the person I would need to help me not only launch these yummy nut butters, but also run the ship in terms of day-to-day operations. Ian Walker, Dave and Wendy's younger brother, had recently moved to Vancouver after a tour of Thailand, Australia and the South Pacific. He was doing what many young people were doing at the time—travelling before they entered the workforce. The four years prior to his trip were spent earning an economics degree, with a specialization in entrepreneurial studies, from Dalhousie University. My presentation evening came and went without much fanfare. With Ian in the crowd for moral support, Ike and I got up in front of my instructors, other industry designers, parents and classmates, and explained how I had come up with not only the name and the look of our packaging but also the nut butters themselves. I had made a batch of the spreads and had them served up on bagels for everyone in attendance.

In the end, the questions were what I would've expected. Why this colour? Why that font? How about that illustration? There wasn't one comment about having Ike on the label. The B-minus letter grade wasn't a surprise and didn't discourage me. All along my goal hadn't been about getting an A but about making a great product with Ike's smiling face on the packaging. I saw the potential of my product as a business venture first, and in my heart I knew Ian and I were onto something. I wasn't about to let my professors ruin the moment.

After two hectic weeks of making nut spreads, labelling them and putting together a display booth, the moment of truth arrived. We were going to be at Granville Island Market for three days— Friday, Saturday and Sunday. Friday morning I set up our booth with Karyn's help. By noon I was barely hanging on, busy laying out samples, answering questions and selling jars—lots of jars. By the end of the day on Saturday, we were sold out—over 200 jars. Skeet & Ike's was a hit.

As Ian and I sat on our porch that evening looking out over the lights of Vancouver, we discussed what possibilities lay ahead. We decided we would take the earnings from the weekend and purchase more ingredients for our next weekend at the market in two weeks' time. After that it would be a one-step-at-a-time process of growing the business. That's exactly what we did for the entire summer— one weekend at the Market followed by two weeks of getting ready for another weekend of sales. Inevitably, as more and more customers encouraged us to branch out, the consideration of getting into stores became something we couldn't avoid.

For Robyn, 1996 was another disappointing year. At the summer Olympics in Atlanta, she failed to qualify for the final of the women's 5,000-metre race after coming down with a bug just before her semi-final. There is nothing worse for an athlete than arriving at a competition perfectly tapered and ready to race, only to get sick in the days leading up to your event. Sometimes it just boils down to bad luck. Given her approach to life, Robyn rebounded quickly and resumed her training for the next season.

By the spring of 1997, Ian and I had managed to build Skeet & Ike's to a point where it attracted private investors whose money would allow us to draw a modest salary and continue growing the company. Shortly after that, sales started to decline because of the ban on peanuts in schools and some unflattering press that resulted in some lean years for many nut-butter manufacturers. Undaunted, we decided to develop a new line of products. After almost two years of doing demos in local grocery stores, one thing Ian and I had both observed was that everyone who came by our table to sample our nut spreads had some form of snack food in their cart, so we decided snack foods were the way to go.

While we were trying to develop a soy nut butter, Ian and I constantly snacked on the roasted soybeans that made up the butter. They were crunchy and satisfying, and one day Ian suggested that we put some seasoning on them and try selling them as a packaged snack. We did just that and within months we were selling in stores all over the Lower Mainland and starting to move across Canada.

For me it was exciting to immerse myself in something challenging again. The fear of failing, or not being the best at this, was a non-issue. We were too small to pose a real threat to anyone, and that provided the safety to go after a new challenge in a new way. As much as I wanted Skeet & Ike's to be successful—to win—I understood that I needed to adapt to a new measure of success: still being in business in a year's time. When we moved from one of the rooms in our house into a new office and manufacturing area closer to the city, we had to accept the fact that all of our hard work was finally beginning to pay off.

By Christmas of that year, Robyn and I were living together, and I figured it was time to speak with Mom about engagement rings. I didn't have the cash to purchase one, so I asked Mom if there was a family ring that just happened to be lying around collecting dust. True to the expression "If you don't ask, you don't get," there was a beautiful diamond ring that was over a hundred years old sitting in Mom's jewellery box. She had inherited it years ago when a relative died. With a little refit and buff, it looked mighty impressive. Because I hadn't discussed marriage with Robyn, I had to give Mom hush orders.

In late August, Robyn returned from her season in Europe, where she had an excellent showing at the 1997 World Championships in Athens. She was the 11th-fastest woman in the world in the 1,500 metres—pretty impressive. The trouble for me was that a national team coach and a friend of ours told me that Robyn had really finished third among the clean athletes. I was shocked. I had been attending track and field events long enough to know that there were some cheaters in the sport but I didn't think it was that bad. Eleventh instead of third because she was clean—to me that was outrageous.

Naturally, my reaction was to ask her the obvious question, "Why bother?" The way I saw it, she was never going to win. The chances of her beating an athlete cranked up on EPO or taking male hormone replacements or steroids was next to nil. "Quit. Go back to school. Finish your degree. Get a job. Start making some money—come on, let's get on with our lives!" was my advice to her. Ironically, this was the same advice I got so upset about when my dad bestowed it upon me.

As usual, Robyn had already thought about it and had decided that she wasn't going to let the choices of her competitors affect her involvement in running. Her answer was that she didn't race to beat those athletes or even win those medals. As uncomfortable as I still was with that, I wasn't surprised. I knew that there would be no changing her mind, so I just accepted that until she had come to the end of her running path, I would do whatever I could to support her.

Later that week I convinced her we needed to go for a little hike up Black Mountain. It was a beautiful day. No clouds—just blue sky and sunshine, with the temperature sitting in the low 20s. After lunch we made our way to the base of the mountain and began our hike. I had made this trek many times because of the Knee Knacker race and I never tired of the beautiful views. It took us about two hours to get to the top, with Ike eagerly leading all the way.

I'd borrowed Wendy's camera earlier in the week and when we got to the top I told Robyn that I wanted to take some pictures of Ike and us. "I'm not sure how this timer works. Can we try a few of these?" I asked.

Trying to be as calm as possible and stop my hands from shaking long enough to work the small dials. Robyn obliged and sat on a nearby rock. I set up the camera, switched on the self-timer, pushed the shutter release and moved to join Robyn as the beeping camera counted down my time to get ready.

CLICK.

"That wasn't so hard. Let's take another one."

I returned to the camera and set it up for another shot. This time I reached in my pouch and made sure the ring was within easy reach. As the beeping began, I hurried back to the rock, grabbing the ring while I sat down. With the camera potentially counting down my remaining life as a single man, I removed my shaking hand from my pouch, turned to Robyn and said, "I was wondering if you would marry me?"

Beep, beep, beep. It was relentless. *Did I add extra seconds to the countdown?*

Robyn turned and looked at me. So began a moment that only a guy can understand and appreciate. A moment when you make public your feelings for someone in the hopes they feel the same way about you. Robyn just looked at me, her beautiful blue eyes staring right into mine.

Holy shit! She looks serious. Hey, Jase, don't hold your breath on this one! It's not lookin' good, buddy.

CLICK.

"Yes. Yes, I will marry you, Jason."

Knowing that the picture was probably not going to be the one I had envisioned—two people jumping up in the air screaming like lovestruck fools, I kissed her.

Screw the picture, Jase. Robyn understands this, the magnitude of what yes means. This is it, buddy! You have just asked someone to spend the rest of her life with you—through thick and thin; in sickness and in health— the whole deal. This isn't a Hollywood movie, Spielberg. It's not about that picture—this is about the two of you stickin' it out together for life.

We tried to get the ring on her finger, but when you've hiked up a mountain, your fingers get a little swollen. We opted for the baby finger until we returned to sea level.

With the Skeet & Ike's cell phone that I had borrowed for the hike, we began calling our respective families to share the news. With 12 siblings between us, parents and a host of friends scattered across the country—it took a while. In fact, we were so busy yakking that we forgot to consider that the setting sun, which was providing a beautiful backdrop to a perfect afternoon, was our only source of light to get back down the mountain—a return trip that could take two hours or more. We had to hustle.

The entire way down was an unending dialogue of what we had just agreed to—the wedding.

Where?

Out here.

How?

Not sure.

Who?

Lots of people.

When?

That was the big question.

7

HEALING

Both of us wanted a summer wedding, but with Robyn still competing, we knew we'd have to wait until she was done running, or another opportunity presented itself. In the meantime, it was an exciting time for both of us. After Robyn's promising showing at that year's World Championships, her fall training was equally as encouraging. By January, the steady progress she'd made set her up nicely for a four-month training camp in Adelaide, Australia. It was an ideal opportunity to generate some solid training with her coach and teammates in a warmer climate. It would enable all of them to return in the spring ready for the upcoming racing season.

Although her time Down Under had been successful, when Robyn returned she started to struggle physically with her training. Less than a week before she left for Europe and her first series of track meets, her blood work came back indicating that she had full-blown mono—her 1998 season was over.

In the meantime Skeet & Ike's was thriving and occupying a good amount of Ian's time, and mine. Even though the company was growing rapidly and I was enjoying a new career path, I was also getting the itch to teach and coach again. In September 1998, I enrolled in UBC's 12-month Bachelor of Education post-degree program. My goal was to return to Shawnigan Lake School to teach art and design, and coach rowing.

That year was busy: attending school during the day, doing homework at night and working for Skeet & Ike's combined for a hectic schedule. As spring approached, I looked forward to the three-month practicum.

For the most part, my first day went smoothly. Even though I wouldn't see "action" until the second week, I was a bit nervous. I spent my days getting to know the students with whom I'd be working for the next few months. I hadn't been in a classroom for a while and, unlike my experience at Shawnigan, these classes were large, and a few of the students had a bit more edge to them. It was going to be a good challenge.

Eventually, my chance to get up in front of the classroom arrived and, at the start of the second week, I began teaching. One afternoon, two of my students thought it would be fun to give the new student teacher a quick lesson on classroom management. We had been told that classroom management wouldn't be our responsibility at the beginning of the practicum and that we could rely on our sponsor teachers to keep their classes in check. When the first shoe went sailing through the air, I stopped and looked at my sponsor teacher to see what he was going to do. He just kept reading the magazine in his lap. When the second shoe launched into the air, I stopped and asked the two guys responsible to leave the class and wait for me out in the hall. I continued with my lesson and got the rest of the class busy with their new assignment and then went to join my new friends. As I came out into the hall, both boys were laughing and joking about their stunt, obviously proud of themselves. When they saw me, the laughing stopped and they gave me a rather unwelcoming look. I let them know that.

"Hey, guys, what makes me the asshole here? You're the ones that threw the shoes."

Neither one of them said a thing.

"I would appreciate it if you could try to be a little less disruptive next time."

Still nothing.

"Okay, head back into the classroom, and let's give this another shot."

The two of them went back inside. Shortly afterward, one of them asked if he could go to the bathroom. He went straight to the principal's office and said that I had called him an asshole.

Within an hour, I was being escorted from the school. My practicum was over, and, in accordance with UBC policy, I was expelled. The next day, a week and a half into my practicum, I found myself meeting with someone from the Dean of Education's office at UBC regarding my future in teaching. Without me knowing it, about 20 of the students had faxed in letters supporting me and saying that the two guys had set out to burn me. I was reinstated at UBC and began my second practicum the next week.

When I showed up to my new school, I was met by an older Dutch gentlemen who had been teaching for many years and obviously knew his way around a high school art room. As we walked together to his first class, he leaned into me and said, "Hey, I heard what had happened at your first school."

"Yeah, that was a bad call," I said looking down a bit embarrassed with myself.

"Ahh, don't worry about it," he returned quickly, "I called my entire class a bunch of assholes last week."

We were going to get along just fine.

After my practicum, I only had my required electives to complete during the summer and everything was set for me to return to Shawnigan. Come September I would be a full-time teacher and coach. All Robyn and I had to do was find accommodation near the school and we were set.

We found a cottage on the lake just a few houses down from the school's main entrance. It was a beautiful piece of beachfront property. We could live there during the school year but would have to move out when the landlord and her family moved back in for the summer. The bonus was she was only going to charge us a few hundred dollars a month in rent—enough to cover her taxes and expenses—in exchange for knowing that someone was taking good care of her cottage during the winter months.

Living in Shawnigan Lake provided Robyn with the ideal opportunity to train on the many wooded trails and old logging roads that surrounded the school. It also allowed her to travel to Victoria to train with her coach and teammates a few times a week.

For Ike life couldn't have been any better. He was living on a lake, and his mom took him on runs with her. His blood work still indicated that his one kidney was doing an outstanding job, and he was thriving as if he were a young dog.

A few months into my teaching, it was apparent that we had landed on our feet and then some. I was enjoying my teaching, my coaching and all of the other duties that came with the job. After a long break from coaching volleyball, I found myself back on the court working with the junior girls' team. Continuing where I had left off 10 years earlier, I made it about having fun and getting better. When the rowing season started up, I tried earnestly to maintain the same outlook but I was assigned the junior girls' crew and, in my attempt to help them "get better," I worked them harder than most were willing to commit to. When our racing season started in the spring, I had whittled the almost forty girls that I had started with down to six. They were a terrific group of girls to work with, though, and they won the silver medal at the National Championships. Not wanting to decimate the girls' rowing program at Shawnigan, the powers that be moved me over to the junior boys' program the following year.

It was now the early summer of 2000 and the Olympic trials were only four weeks away. Robyn's race preparation was at the height of its intensity. The year's training had gone well and her fitness was excellent. As a result, she was running better than she ever had. She and her coach, Wynn Gmitroski, were excited because these Olympics would most likely be her last. Racing in the best shape of her life would be a great finish to a long career.

One Saturday morning Ike and I decided to join Robyn at the UVic track and watch her train. When she finished her warm-up, she started holding her back—something had happened. She and Wynn discussed the pros and cons of continuing the workout so close to the trials. If it was just fatigue, there would be little harm in continuing. If it was a strain, it could potentially end her season.

Robyn and Wynn decided to push on with the prescribed work-out in the hope that running through the discomfort might loosen her back. It seemed to work. In fact, she ran a personal best during one of her timed pieces. At the end of the session, Robyn and Wynn were very excited; things were looking right on track for the Olympic Trials, but as she started her warm-down, her back began to bother her again. Ten minutes into it, she could barely run. I could see from the stands that something was wrong and so I made my way over to Robyn. She was quiet and walking delicately, holding her lower back. I grabbed all of her stuff and helped her to the women's change room. By the time we got there she was struggling to walk and had to lean on me just to make her way to the showers. I helped her undress, manage a quick shower, re-dress and get back to the car. Like most elite athletes, Robyn had a high threshold for pain, but this pain was off the chart.

So began a week of massage, acupuncture, chiropractors and meds. Wynn was Robyn's physio as well as her coach. He assessed her mobility and progress daily. By the end of the first week, she could walk and jog lightly but not train. After another week of the same ritual, she wasn't much better. She was forced to make a decision athletes fear more than anything—withdrawing from the Olympic trials.

I was devastated for Robyn. She had worked so hard, had done everything so right: her training, her diet, everything. She'd left absolutely nothing to chance, only to have a back injury prevent her from going to her third Olympics. All the focus, energy and effort it had taken her to get to this point were for naught. At least, that was my way of looking at it. You train to go to the Olympics to race. It's a finish line in more ways than one, and only when you cross it are you done. Robyn was not going to cross that line this year. She wouldn't feel the excitement of packing to leave for the Games, of landing in Sydney and moving into the Athletes' Village. There would be no opening ceremonies, no television interviews, no pre-race massage and warm-up. She would not have a final word with Wynn before she walked onto the track to get herself set to race. Instead, there would be no race. Robyn's season, possibly her career, was over. That seemed so unfair to me. Of all the runners in the world who should have attended the Olympics that year, Robyn was undeniably one of them. After all, she was clean. As far as I was concerned, she epitomized what the Games stood for. Unlike me, she was the Olympic Creed in living flesh—the most important thing in the Olympics is not to win but to take part. How was this just?

Each morning Robyn woke up and went on with her day, I was dumbfounded. If it had been me? If I had been weeks before my third and last Olympics, at the height of my physical readiness after 16 years of international competition, and an injury had taken away my chance to win an Olympic gold medal, I would have needed surveillance 24 hours a day.

For six years I had listened to Robyn's New Age perspective on racing. Originally I had sneered at the idea, mocked its uncompetitive nature and laughed at its premise every chance I got. Over the years

I had grown to understand it and even admire it. Now, witnessing Robyn's acceptance of her injury, I was sold. There was one reason she was doing so well and that was her perspective. Her cheesy notion of the journey had brought her through this. She was dealing with the otherwise devastating realization of her not attending the Olympics better than anyone I could imagine because she saw her injury and its outcome as part of her journey. And she was now navigating that journey daily. To me, this was more impressive than any Olympic record could ever be. Its impact was immediate—it made me re-think my approach to coaching: how I coached and why I coached. It was a moment of tremendous personal growth for *me*.

As the end of the summer approached, I began preparing for a weeklong workshop on one of the nearby Gulf Islands. For years Fiona had encouraged me to go to the Hollyhock Retreat Centre on Cortes Island and take part in a Heart of the Shaman course. It sounded crazy to me, a lot of self-help phooey: staying up all night long and dealing with evil spirits and the like. Naturally, I considered it to be a load of crap and had brushed off all of her prodding. However, with Robyn not attending the Olympics, we both decided to go.

The first night we experienced a fire-pit ceremony, met everyone and began our journeys of self-discovery. The whole thing pushed me past my comfort level in a big way. I had never done anything even closely resembling this before but Robyn kept reminding me that I had been determined to give it a chance and be open to the process.

The next morning we met in a building that was shaped like a huge teepee. It was filled with all sorts of hippie stuff, like feathers, bones, candles, pictures, etc. I thought it was all weird and flaky, and it was going to take every ounce of patience and restraint I could muster to not only get through this but to not say what I thought of it all.

Everyone sat in a circle and, using what was referred to as a talking stick, something that essentially gave you the floor when you had it, we explained why we were there and what sort of resolution we were hoping for. As a pre-requisite for attending the workshop, we all had to write letters providing some background on our situations, outlining why we were attending. My reason, of course, was that after 12 years I was still pissed off at myself for not winning in Seoul.

I listened as individuals from all over North America shared their stories of despair, tragedy and personal grief. When my turn came, I gave it a pass. Who was I kidding? Amid all of this pain and suffering, I was going to say, "Yeah, hi. My name's Jason and I'm here because I didn't win an Olympic gold medal 12 years ago. Can you help me?" I sat for the rest of the meeting figuring out how I was going to keep my selfish little problem to myself—it was going to be a long week.

Close to four hours later we were finished and headed off to lunch. As I made my way down the steps, one of the facilitators called after me. I turned to face him. His skin was tanned and weathered, his eyes warm, and his smile welcoming.

"Jason. I'm Doug." He put out his hand.

With a firm handshake, I responded, "Hi, Doug, nice to meet you."

"Listen, I read your letter." His eyes looked right inside me.

Oh boy. Here we go. He recognizes the obvious mismatch of my "problem" and the rest of the group. Am I going to be asked to leave?

I just stared at him. I didn't know what to say. *Yeah, we had a bad race—bummer, eh?*

"Believe it or not," he said, "I can relate to what you wrote. I played baseball as a young boy in the States. I'll bet there's only a small percentage of the population who could understand what you've gone through? I'm sorry you've been carrying that around for so long. I look forward to talking with you some more." He put his hand on my shoulder and gave me a subtle understanding nod, and suddenly I felt my guard ease off.

I turned and continued walking down the root-laden path back to the main lodge. Trees surrounded me on all sides. It was a beautiful setting. The warm breeze off the ocean to my right grabbed me, insisting that I stop and look.

Twelve years, Jase. You've been beating yourself up for twelve years. Haven't you had enough? Don't you think it's time to finally let go?

Standing there, feeling that place, I could sense the island knew why I was there. It took hold of my heart and squeezed—hard. As my buried emotions reluctantly oozed out, so too did the tears that ran down my cheeks. I hadn't cried about Seoul since my run in the trails after Canada had won in Barcelona. I hadn't wanted to stir any of it up again. And I was doing okay.

I stuffed my unpacked baggage back down inside and continued along the trail to where lunch was being served. We were told not to overindulge because some of the exercises were going to be strenuous and eating too much could make the experience uncomfortable. But it was hard not to eat too much. Along with all the "spiritual growth" that was going on at this place, they sure knew how to put on a spread. With full and happy bellies, Robyn and I headed for the afternoon session. Two of its facilitators, Richard and Donna, both doctors, had being conducting research for years with a shaman in New Mexico. They had developed a breathing technique that allowed participants to experience something similar to what a traditional shaman would experience using herbs and hallucinogenic drugs. Through repetitive deep breathing, Richard and Donna, could help us come to, for lack of a better term, an altered state. The idea was to go back and deal with past relationships, incidents and any other stuff that might show up.

Needless to say, I was skeptical. *Altered states? Out-of-body experiences? Visions? Ahhh, yah okay.* I was determined to see this through, even if for no other reason than I was going to get my money's worth. I lay down on my mat and started to breathe deeply—I mean really deeply. Huge breaths. One after another. I began to experience some strange things. My hands and fingers curled up like a ball as if someone was pulling my tendons. My neck and back began to arch and my feet began to curl. I was physically uncomfortable and hadn't even started the emotional stuff yet.

In this state of contraction, with my eyes closed, Richard began to talk us through the visual exercises. This is where it got weird. People and places that I hadn't thought of in years began to emerge crystal clear. Scenarios from my past that I would have thought were unimportant and trivial became significant. At certain points it became so intense, so incredibly uncomfortable, that I had to stop and take a break from the physical pain of my entire body being balled up while my mind was taking me places that I hadn't been since the day it happened.

As I went through moments of surprise and wonder with Mom and Dad, past teachers, family and friends, the one person that I expected to show up eventually did. It was Neil, and he was as real as I could have imagined. His svelte physique and his golden soft leathery skin moved exactly as it did in real life when he spoke or smiled. Even his voice was jarringly perfect.

In the weeks leading up to the Olympic Games, Neil and I had struggled with our relationship at times. That summer Neil had been paying particular attention to my length at the catch (how far I was reaching out at the beginning of each stroke, or, more precisely, how far I wasn't reaching out or being short at the catch). Neil would pull up his coach boat beside us during a piece and yell over and over again, "Jason. Don't you dare shorten up at the catch! If you keep doing that I'm going to increase your load. And I'll keep doing it until you stay long out at the front end, goddamn it!" That meant he would increase the resistance when I pulled, making the oar feel heavier.

We would go out for our row the next day and, sure enough, the blade would feel heavier, making it harder to get through the water and keep up with the others. I never understood this tactic; it seemed counterintuitive to improving the length of the stroke. But knowing Neil as I did, I just sucked it up and tried to stay up with the others as best I could. This happened numerous times throughout the summer. Then in Seoul, a week before our first race, he came up to me one more time and said he had loaded me up.

That afternoon, during the row, it was everything I could do to keep up during short 40-stroke pieces. Until then I was determined not to complain. I wanted to prove to him that I could handle anything he threw at me. I was not going to let him break me. But the new load was ridiculous—I wouldn't be able to keep up with the others for 2,000 metres. After the row, I walked straight up to him and said, "You win, Neil. I can't handle that load." As a young boy, I would never have said that to him and certainly wouldn't have continued to glare back at him. But not this time. I was pissed off. He had won. Or so I thought. The next morning I noticed that my load had been eased back.

As the scene played out in my mind, exactly as it had happened that summer, it reignited all of the frustration and anger, and I told him what I would have said to him all those years ago if I hadn't been so frightened.

"You happy? You fuckin' bastard. I don't know what kinda game you're playing at here, but I'm done. You win. That's right. I can't handle that load, Neil. Feel good? Yeah, great, eh? You know what, I'm not a kid anymore. I've grown up. And I've earned the right to sit in this fuckin' boat. So stop treating me like I'm 12. You got a problem with how I'm rowing? Then help me. Don't beat the shit out of me! Do your job and fuckin' coach me."

Neil just stood there and listened. No expression. Nothing. And then I stepped up one last time. "And one more thing. As much as it might make it easier for you to swallow, I'm not the reason we lost."

Shit! Hold on there, Jase.

All these years later, it was still about the loss. My insecurities about being the lightest guy, the last one to make the boat, the little boy in Neil's eyes—they all boiled down to blaming myself for losing that final. No wonder they were still in there.

Over the remaining days of the workshop, similar scenarios played out with Neil, as well as other guys from the boat. The guilt and shame that I felt over losing the race continued to be the focus of each session. By the time the week came to an end, I was absolutely exhausted. My emotions were exposed, raw and bleeding. I had just relived Seoul and everything that I believed it represented to me a thousand times over—enough was enough. I needed for it to be over.

On the final day of the workshop, Richard and Donna recommended that we create some sort of ritual or funeral to let go of whatever we had been holding onto. So that afternoon, right after lunch, I went down to the beach by the ocean and with a broken stick I found laying there I drew the Canadian crest for the national team in the sand—two crossed oars behind a maple leaf. Below that I wrote a line from the speech I had given years ago: *It was my dream and I gave to that dream everything that I had.* I stood back, crouched down and said aloud, "I'm done with you."

Walking back up to the building that had hosted me during the most extraordinary experience of my life, I felt light enough to be blown away in the ocean breeze. When I came out of our final meeting, the tide would have come in, erasing my writing in the sand. That symbolic washing away was to represent the moment I would be finished with all that baggage I had carried with me for too many years.

With September came the Olympics and the usual CBC all-day television coverage. To my amazement, and admiration, Robyn watched everything, including her event. I not only watched the Olympics on TV, I enjoyed them. I was discovering, perhaps for

the first time, the essence of what the Olympics should be about—
the potential of the human spirit. Every time I sat down to watch I
cried, not because someone that I wanted to win had lost or underperformed, but because I realized that someone had stepped onto
the world stage and pushed as hard as they could. It was beautiful
to witness—to experience.

One of the highlights for me was watching the men's eight.
Bryan Donnelly, a member of the Canadian crew, was someone I
had coached at Shawnigan 10 years earlier. I was like a little kid
counting down the days until his first race. In the end, Bryan and
his crew finished seventh, which means they won their petite final,
otherwise known as the second final used to determine the rank-
ings of seventh to twelfth. I was disappointed for the team but only
because I knew they had higher expectations of their final performance, but I was also over the moon proud of what Bryan had done.
He had gone to Olympics to race the best in the world.

When Bryan got home to Canada, I called him up and asked
him to come up to the school to speak to the students and staff about
his Olympic experience. He agreed. Seeing his enormous frame
standing before the students in the chapel two weeks later was a tremendously gratifying moment for me. Here was that skinny little
teenager I had coached all those years earlier, now all grown up. He
was a young man in his twenties who, at 6'7" and 210 pounds, had
reached the pinnacle of amateur sport and was about to pass on the
secret to his success.

Within minutes of Bryan beginning to speak, the entire
chapel was roaring with laughter as he shared the antics of the
opening ceremonies, living in the Athletes' Village and spending
too much time at Bondi Beach with all of the beautiful Aussie
women. Bryan had given me a brief idea of what he was going to
share with the students, but I had no idea that he was going to be
this funny and engaging. I was so happy that the students were

hearing first-hand from an Olympian that the Games were about more than just winning medals.

Bryan was undoubtedly a hit and, I thought, a feather in my cap. But 10 minutes into his talk, Bryan started to share the emotions he'd felt. As he described the buildup to his first race, he mentioned each competing country. His voice grew louder and in an attempt to convey the tension between the boats as they warmed up beside each other in their designated lanes, Bryan's animated gestures reached a climax with a bomb.

"It was a war! It was like a GODDAMN war!"

Holy shit. Tell me he didn't just say that. Bryan, Bryan! Not in the chapel, buddy.

I carefully looked up from my cowering position to see how the Reverend was doing. To my relief, he was not only still sitting upright, but smiling as well. Knowing him as the easygoing padre that he was, I wasn't all that surprised. But I wasn't about to look at our headmaster. There was no way I was going to risk the chance of locking eyes with my boss, a very traditional man whose experience of chapel did not include the word goddamn.

Bryan, on the other hand, seemed oblivious to the whole thing. He continued to rant. "I didn't go over there to lose. I went over there to win."

And that was when I experienced an epiphany, and an ugly one at that. I realized that I was watching and listening to myself when I got back from Seoul. It was undeniable that what Bryan had said and how he had said it—every word and colourful expression—had been a part of my coaching reper-toire 10 years earlier. His philosophy, which he was so willingly sharing now, was what I had instilled in him as his first rowing coach. And it seemed that not one coach after me had changed the message that winning and war, that kicking the crap out of your competitors, were pretty much the industry standard when it came to motivating elite athletes. Bryan was the legacy of all of us.

Arriving home at the cottage, I went straight into our bedroom in search of my old rowing photo album. Flipping to the back, I found the picture from the front page of the *Globe* all those years ago. I hadn't looked at it in years. The pain was still there. The rage and disillusionment. The disgrace. All of it. But along with all that I experienced in that moment was now something new—compassion. I felt compassion for that bitter and angry 24-year-old boy. What a waste—what a complete waste. So much potential had since been crushed by a single-minded approach to success, one based on hating and killing competitors in the pursuit of the ultimate ever-consuming and important goal of winning.

8 ━━━

A NEW WAY OF THINKING

I knew that day that my approach to coaching wasn't going to work for me anymore. I saw that my old archaic, macho approach wasn't going to serve me as a coach and certainly wasn't going to serve my athletes. This photo and all that it represented would no longer be my legacy. I wanted a new and different legacy—a better legacy. If I was going to ensure that, then one thing was for certain—I needed a different message. Because of Robyn, I had seen a different way, a better way. I was determined to use her methods. I decided in that moment I would remove the word *win* from my coaching vocabulary.

I did it. That year, I managed to coach the junior boys' eight and not use the "win" as a motivator for training or racing. And we went fast. The next year, we went faster. I loved it—I was enjoying coaching like I never had before. The guys I was coaching were getting fit and strong, and having fun at the same time. Winning national championships wasn't bad either, I had to admit, but the relationship I was building with these young boys was worth the shift that I had made in my coaching. I knew deep down that my new legacy was intact. That in 10, 15 or 20 years these young guys would remember the challenging training sessions and their teammates more than whether or not they had won.

During this time Robyn and I, with Ike as our ring boy, finally found time to get married. It was the end of the summer of 2001 and Robyn had just finished a frustrating racing season that saw her not qualify for the World Championships. Another year of training had produced more injuries and, after much soul searching, she decided that it was time to listen to her body and not race the 2002 season. Robyn retired from the competitive aspect of running for good.

My original vision for our wedding was that it would be like a three-day camp where family and friends from all across the country travelled to Vancouver Island for a weekend of hiking, running, rowing, swimming, volleyball, pub crawls, the whole gamut. Knowing how much all of this meant to me, Robyn was gracious enough to go along with my plan. As it turned out, it was a lot of work to pull it off, but it was well worth it because everyone enjoyed the beautiful weather and people they hadn't seen in a long while. What had begun seven years earlier as a mission to win her approval and have her as my prized possession had grown into a bond between two friends—a partnership. That summer, we also moved onto the campus to live in what was referred to as the Outpost, an old house at the edge of the property that the school had purchased and fixed up. I was one extremely fortunate man.

In the late spring of 2002, Ike, whom we referred to as our firstborn and who was Robyn's training partner for so many years, died of cancer. It was heart-wrenching to say goodbye to our beautiful boy. In the end, what I found amusing about my relationship with Ike was the irony of how it began. I was supposed to have taught him important lessons so he could become an acceptable guide dog, but it was he who ended up teaching me the important lessons of unconditional love, trust, loyalty and patience so I could become a better person.

At the end of the 2003 school year, the senior boys' rowing coach at Shawnigan left and, after applying, I got the job. I had mixed emotions. I was excited about the challenge, but I was concerned about whether my new approach to coaching the juniors would be effective at the senior level. Coaching 14- and 15-year-old boys was one thing; working with 16-, 17- and 18-year-old young men was a whole new game. Senior rowers, like so many other senior-level athletes, take their results more seriously. Schools garner international recognition based on how well their rowing crews do, and Shawnigan was no different.

The unwritten expectation of my new post was performance. The school had never won a national championship in the senior eight event, and it had been years since a Shawnigan crew had even won the senior eight race at its own regatta. My understanding was that they were hoping that I might change that.

Part of the attraction of coaching the senior team that year was knowing that I would have fun continuing to work with these guys. Over the three years that I had worked with them as juniors, we had become good friends. As seniors, training would begin in September and we would have a three-hour chunk of time each day to laugh and joke around. To have this with a group of teenagers, who were as keen as I was about going fast, was my idea of a dream job. Training and hard work aside, I knew it was going to be a great year.

Jesse, the boys' captain of rowing, had rowed for me as a junior for two years and for the previous coach for one year. He wasn't the biggest guy in the group, but he was tough as nails, and he rowed well. The other great thing about Jesse was that he was a natural leader. Although he didn't pull the highest ergometer score and wasn't the strongest guy in the weight room, he commanded the respect of every guy on the team. One of the key roles of a good stroke is being a coach's conduit to the crew off the water. When Jesse spoke, the others listened. He understood fully what I expected from him and the others and knew what it would take to achieve that. Naturally, I was thrilled to be working with him again. We both wanted the same thing—to go fast and have a fun year doing it.

On the first day of school, I met with all 14 rowers down at the boathouse. I explained that I wanted to maintain the same culture; we wouldn't use the word *win* when we discussed training or racing. Instead, quite simply, the goal of the year was to show up at the national championships and race to the best of our abilities. If we could do that, it would be a successful year.

I went on to explain that they were going to put in more miles in the next nine months than they ever had before so that they would arrive in St. Catharines in the best racing shape of their lives. "The way I see it," I said, "is that we have two things we can have an effect on—our fitness and our technique. So those are the two areas we'll focus on. And, that's it."

I paused for a moment—making sure they were hearing what I meant. "The priority boats this year will be the eight and then the quad. That means the eight fastest guys will sit in the eight, and nine through twelve will sit in the quad. How hard you work between now and June 6th will determine which boat you sit in. No seats are set—they're all open, and each of you has an equal shot at the top boat. Even the novice guys—it might be a little harder but it's possible. If you come down here every day and work your ass off, anything is possible. Is that understood?"

Apparently it was; no one spoke up.

Of the novices who showed up, one in particular caught my attention. He was a big kid who had come down with one of the experienced guys.

"What's your name?" I asked him.

"Travis," he replied with a friendly smile and welcoming posture. I had taught enough teenagers to know right from the start that this young fellow was void of attitude. I liked him already.

"Where ya from?" I said, thinking he had to be from a farm somewhere on the prairies to be this polite.

"Calgary."

"Ah, Cowtown. I have some good friends from there. It's a fun city. Why did you come down here today, Travis?" I wanted to know if I had keeper.

"I heard Pat talking about it last night. He said rowing was intense and a lot of work, but it sounds fun," he said almost bashfully.

"Yeah, in a weird sort of way I guess, it is kinda fun. Well, you keep showin' up and we'll see what we can do to make it as fun as possible."

The next day, we put together some lineups and went out for our first row. Before we left the dock, I explained that I wanted to try a new technique this year. Mike Spracklen had found success with the Canadian national team men's eight over the previous few years, winning a number of World Championships. He was using a longer layback position (sitting with legs flat and body leaning toward the bow) with his crews, which meant that instead of carrying the body through to a finish position that would have the shoulders just past the hips, he had his athletes taking their shoulders back a foot farther or more.

Whereas most people saw it as just a longer layback, I saw it as an opportunity to lengthen the acceleration phase of the stroke. Canadians weren't always known for their size on the international stage, and this adaptation allowed Spracklen to get the most out of each of his athletes. It made sense to me, and if it was good enough for Spracklen, then it was good enough for us.

Starting that afternoon, we began extending our finish positions to ensure we had a longer acceleration phase, the key to executing this model properly. It wasn't good enough to just lay back further; you had to continue to accelerate the blade in the water. As Spracklen would say, "You have to contribute to boat speed." What he meant by that was, that if your blade was in the water and it wasn't helping the boat go faster, then it was helping the boat go slower and that wasn't good. So we worked hard to ensure that each part of the stroke, especially the finish, contributed to boat speed.

It took a few rows, but within a week or two, everyone got the hang of it and the boats were moving along quite well. By the end of September we were putting in 16-kilometre rows of decent quality, and we were getting fitter and faster with each outing. Things were going well; it was time to see exactly what we had.

Brian Carr was now the head of rowing at Brentwood College. His dad, Tony Carr, had just retired after a winning run with an exceptional crew he had during the early part of the new millennium. Brian had taken over from his dad and had inherited a senior boys' program that needed some rebuilding. Almost an entire crew had graduated and gone on to row at various prestigious American colleges.

I had known Brian since my days at UVic, where he had been the lightweight coach. Before he started coaching, he had rowed as a lightweight, almost cracking the national team in 1985. He coached like the typical lightweight rower he had been—scrappy, competitive as hell and tenacious in his pursuit of more boat speed. All of that aside, he was a good guy who enjoyed getting together for beers and sharing old rowing stories. I was genuinely looking forward to coaching up the road from him.

One of my goals for the year was to demystify the whole Shawnigan–Brentwood rivalry. I liked Brian and I had a lot of respect for him as a coach, so I wasn't going to encourage, or condone, any bad mouthing of him or his athletes. It was my goal to create a new culture between our schools, one in which the athletes not only knew each other but got along. If there was one thing I had learned, hating your competitor was no way to motivate yourself.

We were going to find bigger reasons to go fast. I knew Brian was of the same mind; there was no reason why the guys couldn't be friends and still race hard against one another. I made a phone call to Brian. We made plans to have the crews meet up later that week at Brentwood. In typical Brian fashion, he had a loaner boat rigged, ready and waiting by the time we got there. He took time to introduce all of his athletes. As they shook hands for the first time, they were polite but quiet.

Brian and I decided on a workout and then proceeded to get our crews ready. Just before we went out on the water, I pulled everyone in. "Now, just like we've been doing back home, when we go out there, we focus on what's going on in our boat—not theirs. I don't want to see anyone looking over at the Brentwood crew. Just focus on your own stuff. Don't misunderstand me, this is a race—each piece is a race. But to go faster than them, you have to take care of your own business. Okay?"

Quiet—they were dead quiet.

"Now, go out there and mess up that water—ya got it?"

Jesse nodded. With that I knew they were ready.

I shoved them off and went over to the dock to join Brian where the coach boats were tied up. As I put on my life jacket and continued catching up on how things were going at Brentwood, I noticed a huge mass of a man bounding down the walkway to join us. That frame and stride could only belong to one person—Marius Felix. He had left Shawnigan a few years earlier and I'd missed having him around. I could always count on him for a good laugh and a big hello when I would pass him between classes. He was now working at Brentwood and had wanted to come out and watch the two crews practise together. It was great to see him again.

Travis was the fourth passenger in the boat. I had brought him with us so that he could get a sense of what rowing was all about. He had stuck it out so far and was doing quite well. I wanted him to see close up what it was like to go head-to-head with another crew. If he was feeling up to it at the end of the practice, I might even put him in for a short piece.

When the two crews were ready, we pulled up beside them and shut off the motor. It was a beautiful September day. Brentwood's picturesque campus looked stunning in the autumn light. With Mount Baker and the Coast Mountains shining in the background, the Shawnigan boys greeted Marius. Their eager hellos were a testament to the connection he had made with them during his time at the school.

Brian explained the workout to both crews, and with everyone ready, we got underway. As the two boats paddled side-by-side, Brian grabbed his megaphone and yelled out to the boys. "In two strokes. In one. On the next stroke, away you go!"

In most cases, when two crews are going to race against each other during a practice, it is the coxies' job to keep the competing crews even and await the start of the piece. Any coxie worth his weight never waits for that third stroke to start the piece. They get their boat to jump right on the first stroke, trying to take advantage of any opportunity to get a quick lead on the other crew.

Alex Tay, known as Tay since we had two Alexes on the team, was our coxie. He was an essential part of the boat. Like Jesse, he was smart. He understood the importance of restraint, patience and a good dose of social grace when trying to work with big athletes who could be quick to anger. He had coxed my junior crew the previous year and done a good job. Technically he still had a few things to work on, but his love of going fast more than made up for any shortcomings. As a rower there was nothing better than hearing sincere excitement in a coxie's voice in the middle of a race. However, underneath his feisty competitive streak was a calm communicator. Tay got into racing position like a good jockey—hunched over as he barked encouragement to his crew. He had come to race and was now, along with his eight horses, slowly pulling away from the Brentwood crew.

Watching Jesse race was a sight to behold. His face was expressionless, but the intensity with which he went after each stroke was palpable. A few minutes into the piece, Marius leaned into me and asked me over the roar of the motor, "Is that Jesse in your stroke seat?" I nodded. "He sure likes to pull." That was saying something coming from Marius. I smiled approvingly. I knew that with Jesse in that seat, my choice not to focus on winning that year was made much easier. Deep down, I wanted to win—badly—but I wanted to prove that I could coach a crew without using the win as the focal point of our motivation and still be successful.

After a few pieces I could see the two returning members of Brian's crew getting frustrated. They weren't used to losing pieces to anyone. Even as juniors they had won every regatta they had ever entered. Now, for the first time in their rowing careers, they were experiencing defeat and, understandably, not enjoying it. As we pulled up to the two crews, Brian tried to light a fire under some of the newer members of his crew who hadn't quite figured out what it meant to go after a piece with everything you had.

I looked over at Jesse and quietly asked, "How's it going?" He nodded assuredly. That was about as good as it got with Jesse. If he wasn't pleased he'd be saying so.

Then, I looked at Travis in our boat. He had a big-ass grin lingering on his face.

"What do think?" I asked.

"Awesome! That looks like so much fun," he said, seemingly about to burst out of his skin.

"Do you want to get in there and give it a shot?"

His face went blank. "Right now?"

"No, tomorrow. Of course right now, ya big goof!" I smiled, trying to reassure him that he could do this. "Look, just get in there and do your best. Don't worry about pulling too much at first. Just get the hang of it. When you feel comfortable, try to put a little juice on the end of your oar. You'll be fine. Come on, you can do this." I motioned for him to get ready.

We pulled up beside my crew and switched him into the boat. As Brian put the motor in reverse, we backed away from the boat, leaving Travis to tie up his shoes and get ready, I looked over at Tay and smiled. "Take it easy on him."

When they began rowing, Travis looked lost; it was a case of sensory overload. Asking him to jump in there mid-workout was a lot. He had only been rowing for a few weeks and here he was sitting in the middle of the senior boys' crew about to go head-to-head with Brentwood, but with each stroke he relaxed a little more. It wasn't long before he was following the rest of the crew and even sending down a decent-sized puddle. He was doing just fine for a first go at it. By the end of the workout he was all smiles—he was hooked.

With everyone on the bus, I thanked Brian for having us down for the afternoon.

"Hey, our pleasure, Jase. That was worthwhile. Let's do that again."

"Yeah, that was good—I'm glad we did it." Not sure how to ask my next question because of the assumption that came with it, I hesitated. "Listen, Brian, I was thinking of taking the guys to Henley this year. What do you think—are they fast enough?" Even though I knew how positive and supportive Brian always tried to be, I knew he wouldn't bullshit about this.

"Oh yeah, you got some speed there. I would definitely consider it," he said, nodding his head. I paused for a second, letting Brian's answer sink in. *Holy crap! I had better not screw this up.*

"Okay. Thanks, again, Brian. Let's keep in touch." I shook his hand one more time and jumped onto the bus. My head was spinning, and my stomach beginning to knot, as I entertained the notion of what Henley could mean.

Henley Royal Regatta was the most prestigious regatta in the world. It ran every July on the Henley-on-Thames regatta course—it didn't get much better than 2,112 metres of dual-style racing. The event that we could enter was the Princess Elizabeth Challenge Cup. The top crews from Europe, Great Britain, Australia, the United States and Canada travelled thousands of miles to vie for the title of fastest high school crew in the world. Henley held a special place for me. My brothers, Scott and then Paul, had gone and won there when they were at Ridley during the 1970s.

In 1973, the *Toronto Star* had done an article on Neil's eight that year, the crew to which Scott belonged. The headline had read, "So Good, They Were Called Unfair." They had done it in classic Neil Campbell style, with a commanding lead, and had set a course record.

The same expectations were placed on Paul's boat in 1977. When they were out on the course in the days leading up to the regatta, they came upon the crew from Hampton Grammar School, England. When Hampton saw the enormous size of the Canadians, they began to laugh at the absurdity of being matched against this boatload of high school apes. Hampton and Ridley would eventually meet in the final, and Ridley would win.

Nineteen eighty-two was supposed to be my year to go and, hopefully, win. If we were victorious, our family would have become the first to have three siblings win the event. As usual, Neil felt that we had to win the Canadian Championship to earn the right to go. He wasn't about to take a crew over there if they weren't, at the very least, the fastest crew in Canada. We came third in the final that year to Brentwood and Atlantic City, an American crew. After our final, Neil drove us back to the school. It was a quiet ride. Everyone dealt with the loss in their own way. Mine was anger. As we pulled into the school, Neil told me to wait behind. Then, with me sitting in the passenger seat, he said, "I know how much going to Henley this year meant to you, but we're just not fast enough. There's no way I'm going to go over there and risk getting knocked out in the early rounds. There's no way." He reached up and squeezed the back of my neck—his trademark. "I know it's shitty, Jase. But do you understand why?"

Twenty years later, sitting on that bus with another opportunity to go, but now as a coach, I completely understood why. The amount of time, energy, resources and money it would require to take a crew overseas was astounding. If the chances of getting through to the final weren't good from the get-go, then it would be classified as what we used to call "a trip and a tracksuit."

"So what did Brian have to say?"

I turned around. It was Max, or Big Max as we referred to him. We had two Max's on the crew that year, and we differentiated them by their physical size. Like Jesse, I had coached Big Max as a junior in Grades 9 and 10. He had rowed the previous year in the senior program and now we had one year left together. Big Max was, in a word, intense. He trained hard. He raced hard. He loved going fast. He was one of the reasons we had so much speed. Although his intensity could rub some of the other athletes the wrong way, I appreciated it. At times, I saw myself in his single-minded pursuit of getting stronger and faster. As a teenager, Friday and Saturday nights were my opportunity to get ahead of my competition. I always figured that no one else would be training at that time, so I did. Max was of the same cloth. If hard work was good, then harder work was better.

"He appreciated us coming down for the row. He's knows he's got some work to do and that was about it."

"Yeah, but what did he say about us?" Max wasn't giving up that easy.

"He thought we had some decent speed." Max smiled at me knowing there was more. "That's all we talked about. We're going to try to get together more often. That's it."

The next day I went to see Peter Yates, now Director of Athletics at Shawnigan and, more importantly, still my first choice when I had something on my mind. I told him about our practice with Brentwood and Brian's comments afterwards, and that I was now considering Henley. He was excited at the prospect of a Shawnigan Lake crew going overseas after such a lengthy hiatus. As predicted, he gave me a long list of items to consider and people to contact in England. He reminded me that with travel the way it was now, post-9/11, getting on travel plans sooner rather than later was a good idea. He also pointed out the obvious first stop that I hadn't considered. I needed to run this by our headmaster, Dave Robertson, which I did directly after my meeting with Peter.

With Dave on board, I phoned Peter's contacts in England and got the trip rolling. It was happening; each day I knocked a few more things off my list. I told my rowers that Henley was on the table because the eight was moving well, but we still had seven more months of training ahead of us. We had to be fast enough to go. We had to earn it.

With the end of November approaching, our training was progressing as well as I could have hoped. An average week saw us putting in several 20-kilometre rows along with weight room and ergometer sessions. The guys were becoming fit and strong. Spracklen's technique adaptation was now simply the way we rowed; it was no longer something we were learning.

Each afternoon I would make my way down to the boathouse with my new coaching companions, Katie, a sweet yellow Lab cross, and Benson, a beautiful Akbash-golden retriever cross, both recent additions to our family. It was my favourite time of the day—a chance to hang out with my dogs on a picturesque lake and work with eager young athletes. In many ways, I saw coaching as similar to being an artist—in this case, a sculptor. I'd begun with an enormous lump of clay and each day I showed up and cut away, added to and moulded it into the most powerful, balanced and beautiful piece of work that I could.

I loved it.

9 ▸━━━━━

A NEW TEAM OF HORSES

On the Monday of our last week of hard training before the Christmas holidays, I arrived to set up the ergometers for the workout. When I arrived at the boathouse, Jesse was standing by the door. We walked into the erg room together, and as we did I got a big whiff of pot.

"You smell that?" I paused and looked at Jesse. I took another sniff. "It smells like pot in here."

"I don't smell anything," was Jesse's response.

I continued to the back of the room to put down my stuff and get the room ready for the workout. I turned and looked at Jesse. He was now sitting on the erg, starting to warm up, but he wouldn't look at me in the huge mirrors that stood directly in front of him and which reflected the embarrassed look that was growing on his face.

As the others rowers arrived, I asked them if anyone could smell anything. They all said they could smell pot. My heart started to race and my stomach began to knot. I knew Jesse had been busted for smoking dope when he was in Grade 9, but I had chalked that up to youthful experimentation.

Throughout the entire session, every time I looked at Jesse, he looked away. Something was wrong and I had to find out what. At the end of the workout, I walked up to him.

"Do we need to talk?" I asked.

Jesse nodded. "We do. Can I come out to your place tonight around nine?"

We looked at each other, knowing this wasn't going to be good. After tidying up the ergs, I began my 10-minute walk home. In my head I raced through every scenario I could imagine. From good to bad to unbelievable, I went through them all. When I got home and told Robyn, she calmed me down and told me just to hear him out, but I could feel my anxiety building.

What the hell was I going to do? Jesse was undoubtedly the main reason the team was progressing as fast as it was. His impact on the other athletes in the boat was what any coach would want. He was a born leader and if we lost him we would be in huge trouble. The thought that Jesse, the young man I had coached from the age of 14, a young man who had won national championships and who had dreamed about going to Henley, was now recklessly playing with something that could jeopardize our plans was more than I wanted to entertain.

After three agonizing hours, the doorbell finally rang. I offered Jesse something to drink and we sat down in the living room. Sitting there looking at each other, I knew I didn't want to have this conversation. I didn't want to know. I just wanted to forget it and move on. I couldn't, though; I was more than just a teacher and a coach at this school, I was responsible for things far beyond teaching art and coaching rowing. I was supposed to step in when circumstances warranted it, and these did.

"So, Jesse. What happened down there today?"

When the answer I feared came, I felt confused, angry and betrayed. When there was a long enough break, I asked the obvious question, "Where do we go from here, Jesse?"

"I'm not sure. I'm guessing you have more to do with that than I do at this particular juncture."

He was right. At that moment I had to decide how it would play out. I could simply tell him that it was going to be between him and me, and we would move on and forget about it. We would show up for practice tomorrow and no one would have to know what had transpired. That would be the easiest and cleanest way out.

"Have you spoken with anyone? Does Mark know about this?"

Mark was the one of the assistant headmasters at the school. He was also Jesse's academic advisor. His decorated career as a national team rugby player and his ambitious approach to life made him the perfect mentor for Jesse. They had a good relationship, and if anyone would know how to proceed, it would be him.

"No. I haven't talked to anyone," replied Jesse.

"I'm going to call him and suggest that you stop in at his house on your way back. The two of you can chat about this. Okay?"

"Okay." He stood up, made his way to the door and began putting on his boots and jacket while I phoned Mark.

After a quick exchange, I hung up and turned to face Jesse. "He'll wait up."

I opened the door and the two of us stepped out onto the porch.

"Well, I really don't know what's next, Jesse. Hopefully Mark does. Thanks, for coming out. I'll see you tomorrow."

The black winter's night quickly swallowed Jesse as he made his way down our gravel driveway. I stood on the cold wooden porch in my stocking feet, watching my breath dance in the freezing December air, illuminated by our single outdoor light. The sound of the gravel grinding under Jesse's feet grew softer as he walked in darkness along the path toward Mark's house.

I opened the door and walked back inside. Robyn came down and took my hand. "How are you doing?"

"I don't know," I answered. "I really don't know. I feel numb. I adore that guy. But at this moment I'm really pissed at him. There's so much on the line here, Robyn. How could he do this?"

"What did he have to say?" she asked quietly.

"You know what? I'm not sure. I was so busy going over scenarios in my head, I don't remember much of what he said. He's gone to Mark's to talk with him about what happened. Who knows where things will go from there."

"I know you're upset with Jesse right now," she said. "And you're wondering about the future of your crew, but if you can find some compassion for him and trust that everything will sort itself out the way it's meant to, this will be much easier."

As much as I knew Robyn was right, I hated the notion of trusting. I still needed to be hurt and mad for a while.

Walking into school the next morning, Mark's office was my first stop. As I approached his door, I could see him sitting across from Jesse, and neither one was smiling. When Jesse saw me through the window, he looked away.

When Mark saw me, he gestured that he would come out and join me in the hall. "Well, our young friend has made a big mistake here, Jason." Mark looked serious, but he was calm. On the outside, he was doing better than I was.

"What does that mean?" I was now beginning to panic.

"Jason, this is Jesse's second offence regarding smoking pot here at the school."

"Okay?"

"What that means is that he's being expelled. He'll head home in a few hours and, as of right now, he's not coming back after Christmas."

"Oh shit. Mark, you gotta be kidding?" I was beginning to feel nauseated. What had I done?

"Believe me, I wish I was. I don't want to lose Jesse any more than you do. But the school's policy on this is clear. A second offence smoking pot and you're gone."

"Yeah, but that was three years ago, Mark. Come on, he's in his last year. A suspension I can understand, but kicking him out?"

"Listen, I know this is crappy, but if we bend the rules for Jesse, then every parent of every kid who ever got kicked out for smoking dope is going to be phoning us up complaining. We can't have different rules for Jesse."

I could appreciate Mark's position, and the look in his eyes said he was not enjoying this one bit. The school's decision was undoubtedly proving to be equally as challenging for him. I also heard the logic in his answer. He was right; there was no way to change this. I had nothing to say.

"Do you want talk to him?" Mark asked.

I nodded.

As I walked into Mark's office to join Jesse, all the anger I had built up was gone. In an instant it had washed away, replaced with an overwhelming feeling of guilt and sympathy. Guilt for having busted him and sympathy for the reality that had to be setting in for Jesse. Shortly, he would be going home and, most likely, not returning, which meant he would not attend his graduation ceremonies with all of his friends and peers in June. He wouldn't stroke the eight at the national championships or accompany us to Henley. Beyond that, he would lose his recently awarded scholarship to an Ivy League school. Within 24 hours, Jesse's future had changed drastically.

Sitting on the stiff leather couch, he was quiet and his expression was empty.

"How are you doing?" seemed the easiest way to begin the conversation.

"Okay," was his response.

"Have you talked to your folks?"

"Yeah, they know. They're not too thrilled."

In silence, we sat there conversing in our minds.

"I don't really have any wise advice at this moment, Jesse."

"Yeah. That's okay. I don't imagine it would change much."

The safety of silence returned once again. My heart went out to him. I couldn't imagine what was going on in his world. However, the underlying question that kept coming up for me was *why*. With so much on the line—why take the risk? Besides that, he was the stroke of the heavy eight. There's no doubt that he understood that smoking anything might compromise his ability to do his job properly. Jesse was not stupid, not by any means. He would have understood that smoking pot wasn't going to help our quest. Now, because of his choice to get high, his world, his teammates' world and my world was turned upside down. And with that internal dialogue, my anger came.

"Jesse, I know I'm stating the obvious here. But when the light turns red and you choose to step out into traffic, there's a good chance you'll get hit. What were you thinking?"

At that point, Mark came back into the room. Not wanting Jesse to have to answer my question in front of Mark, I stood up. I turned to face Jesse. "If I don't get to see you, I'll say goodbye now." I put my arms around him and gave him a hug. I could feel his fear. For the first time in our relationship, I could sense that he was scared. "You take care of yourself, Jesse. I'll call you at home." With that, I walked off to class.

When I arrived at the art room, a student came running up to me. "Is it true that Jesse is getting kicked out for good?" More students gathered around, eager to hear my response.

"Look. Just get out your work and let's get started on our projects. Okay?"

When I ran into each of the other guys in the crew throughout that morning, their mood was sombre. Yet, each wanted to know if we were still rowing that day.

The more often I got asked that question, the more it bothered me. "What do you think?" I snapped. "Of course we're rowing. Same time. Same everything."

Jesse was undoubtedly a key member of the boat and by no means could I deny the impact he had had on the crew and our success so far. The other guys not only respected him and looked up to him, but they adored him as well. That didn't mean we could pack it in. We were by no means done. We still had exceptional athletes and we would keep going, keep training in the hopes of getting faster. I wasn't about to let the loss of one guy, however significant he was, sink the program.

What made me even angrier was when another coach came up to me in the staffroom and said, "Jason, that's too bad about Jesse. I'm sorry about that. It must have been hard to make that call. You know, to turn him in? I mean, I don't think I would have done the same. Shows good character on your part." I couldn't believe my ears.

Good character? It had nothing to do with my character, believe me. I thought I was doing my job. Are you saying that you would have protected your athlete if the same had happened to you? How dare you tell me that now!

That afternoon I had Evans, the freshman coach from Yale University, show up to have a look at some of my athletes. He was on a recruiting trip to the US Pacific Northwest and had taken the opportunity to jump across the border and check out a few Canadian schools. For the first half of the year, when these American coaches weren't working with their current crop of rowers, they were securing the future of their program by trying to snag as many of the continent's top high school rowers as they could for the following year's season.

Evans seemed like a good guy; he was young and keen to develop fast crews back home in New Haven, Connecticut. He mentioned that Rush was one of his favourite bands, a good strategy for anyone visiting Canada, especially given I was a huge Rush fan. We shared some Rush concert stories and talked about our favourite albums as we waited for my rowers to show up at the boathouse for practice. Our small talk proved useful in avoiding the huge elephant in the room—Jesse.

That was, until the crew began to show up, some of them noticeably upset.

Evans spoke up. "Listen, I heard about your strokeman."

"Yeah. Not a good situation there."

Finally, Tay arrived. "Hey, Dorland, a lot of the guys are still back at their houses. They say they don't feel like rowing today."

I apologized to Evans and quickly walked off to speak with them. They were all gathered in one of their rooms, some of them crying. They were hurting more than I had anticipated, but we still had to row.

"Look, I know what happened to Jesse was shitty," I began. "And believe me, I feel horrible about my involvement in how it went down, but we have to keep moving forward. Yes, you're pissed about this, and I can appreciate that, but there's a coach here from Yale who has come up to watch you guys row. It would be a drag if he didn't get to see you in action. I'll give you a few minutes to get sorted out, but then let's get out on the water for a short paddle. Okay?"

Over the next few days, I found out some important new information about Jesse. He had seen some doctors and psychiatrists who had determined that he was using pot to self-medicate for a condition that manifested as a loud buzzing sound in his head that got louder with each day unless he smoked to alleviate it. He was using the marijuana to manage the discomfort and accompanying anxiety he was experiencing. To do that, he was biking a considerable distance off campus by himself when he felt he needed relief. He was not smoking dope at parties or in a social manner with any of the other students. To Jesse, it was not about getting high, it was about survival.

When the students got wind of this, they wanted a meeting with the administration to ask if they could reconsider Jesse's expulsion. Given the new information regarding the contributing circumstances around Jesse's choice to smoke, they felt Jesse's punishment warranted a fresh look. I attended the meeting. The students presented an impassioned plea for Jesse. They felt that he should be allowed to return to the school to finish off his year. The administrative staff explained the school's position and how changing their minds now would create the undesirable optics of "moving the goalposts" to let Jesse return. The students weren't thrilled with the explanation, and neither was I.

By the end of that week, the term was finally over and the campus was empty. All of my rowers had left for their Christmas break. Before they did, I explained that when they returned from the holiday we needed to move on and focus our energy on getting back to some productive training. I reminded them of what Neil used say to us during the long winter months of indoor training: "This is when you find your boat speed. Not a week before your race, not a month before, but seven months before. There's no such thing as cramming for a rowing race."

I gave them their workout schedules for the three weeks they would be away and wished each a safe trip home and some relaxing time with their families. They needed it. Shawnigan, like so many other independent schools, was no picnic. It was a pressure cooker, and the bar was always set high, in all respects—academically, athletically, artistically and socially. They had to be on their toes at all times. They were expected to maintain a demanding pace, but it served a purpose. More than preparing them for university life, it allowed them to explore their potential in so many areas. I was always amazed at some of the student transformations that occurred because of the structure and workload that governed their lives. Some students arrived delinquent and lost, and left as accomplished young adults ready to take on anything.

School holidays, especially the Christmas one, were also a chance for the staff to recharge their batteries. The challenging pace that the students kept was no easier for the staff. It was a tough gig. We were constantly reminded that teaching at Shawnigan was more than a job—it was a lifestyle.

It was lifestyle that I loved. Teaching at Shawnigan was about being a part of something bigger than me. The sense of community that existed was both comforting and inspiring. I liked knowing the students well. It was what I had grown up with at Ridley—it was what I knew. There was no "teacher versus student" mentality—everyone was in it together. And, for the most part, people looked out for each other.

It was a great job, but between 25 and 30 hours of coaching a week plus teaching, plus working for Skeet & Ike's, I was pretty busy. That was a lot of time when I wasn't at home with Robyn. Thankfully, we didn't have children—yet. As our holiday began, I told myself that I was going to try to forget about rowing for a few weeks and really enjoy some downtime with Robyn. On many occasions throughout the fall, she had waved her hand in front of my face at the dinner table, saying, "Hello, Jason. Come in off the water," in an attempt to engage me in conversation.

I admit I had a lot on my mind. I was constantly thinking about how my guys were doing—academically, socially and physically. Were they keeping up with their homework? Were they staying out of trouble? Most importantly for me, were they handling the training okay? Was it too much? Was the volume of work I was giving them pushing the boundaries for some of them, particularly the novices? Was I pushing them to race faster so I could live vicariously through them? Or was it just because I wanted to prove to myself and other rowing coaches that we didn't have to create a culture solely focused on winning and killing our competitors to motivate our athletes, either at the junior or the senior level, to be their best?

Two days into the break, my plans for a rowing-free holiday, however well intended, were proving more challenging than I had originally thought. For one thing, I couldn't stop thinking about the new information that had materialized about Jesse. As much as I told my guys that we had to move on, I wasn't doing that myself. That morning Peter phoned and suggested that we set up a meeting with Mark to propose an alternative to expelling Jesse.

In typical Peter fashion, he had another way of looking at things. He saw the present circumstances involving Jesse as an opportunity to create a new, different and progressive resolution. His idea was to bring Jesse back to the school in January, thereby allowing him to finish his year at Shawnigan and all that that entailed, and in return he would be like a student counsellor working with other Shawnigan students who had also been busted for smoking pot.

I thought it was a brilliant idea, an opportunity for the school to acknowledge that yes, they were moving the goalposts mid-game, but with warranted reason, given the circumstances, and for a potential positive effect on other students.

As I hung up the phone, I was running through the possibilities of what this could mean. Of course I wanted to get my stroke-man back, but I also sincerely wanted Jesse to finish his time at Shawnigan on a positive note. I shared Peter's proposal with Robyn, and she also thought the idea, if accepted, made for a win-win situation. She was studying for her master's in counselling psychology at the University of Victoria at the time and saw Peter's idea as not only progressive, but the next logical step in Shawnigan becoming a leader in education with regard to how schools dealt with student drug use.

We met with Mark the next day and proposed Peter's idea. Mark appeared to understand the premise of what Peter was suggesting, but he was still getting stuck around the inconsistency of the school's policy on drug use and the potential damaging optics of changing the rules to allow a star pupil and athlete back into the school.

Knowing Mark was genuinely struggling with this decision, I said I appreciated his concerns, but I still believed that kicking

Jesse out was the wrong decision. He had attended the school since Grade 9. His parents had entrusted his well-being to us, and in doing so, he had become a thriving member of the Shawnigan Lake School family. Now, it seemed that when he needed our support and understanding the most, we were letting him down. At a time when he needed our unconditional love, we were abandoning him, and I saw that as an ultimate act of betrayal. Mark promised to get back to us the next day. Not surprisingly, the administration's decision was final. Jesse would not be returning in January.

As we resumed training a few weeks later, my rowers were focused once again. Everyone seemed to have processed Jesse's situation and realized there was nothing more they could do. Knowing full well there was no way I could replace Jesse on the team, I looked for a new strokeman.

Breaking up the eight and practising in two coxed fours allowed me to try out the candidates more quickly. Every day we tried new combinations in each of the boats, desperately trying to recapture the speed we had harnessed prior to Christmas. It was a slow and sometimes frustrating process, but the encouraging reality was that we were making progress. What became clear was that our goal of going as fast as we could at the national championships in June was helping us manage this enormous hurdle. Each of these athletes had been knocked down hard by the news about Jesse. They had lost their stroke—a key member of the crew, their captain, their leader and, above all, their friend—but they were getting back up, brushing themselves off and starting all over again. They had realized that *we* still existed and, therefore, *we* could still go as fast as *we* could on June 6th. Instead of dwelling on the loss of a teammate, and the potential negative effect that would have had on their chances of winning, they chose to identify what we needed most—to figure out our best lineup. And that meant showing up to each practice committed to helping each other find new physical and mental limits.

This crazy notion of not focusing on the win was actually saving us from frustration and failure.

To start with, we tried Big Max in stroke seat, but not only was he physically too heavy, he was also too fiery and too impatient. A good stroke recognized that he had to be tolerant and work with the athletes behind him—to know when to bite and when to praise. All Big Max knew was how to bite, which is what made him so good at doing his job, which was pulling.

Pat Jocelyn was another big strong athlete who had rowed for me two years earlier as a junior with Big Max and Jesse. He was back for his final year as a senior rower, hoping to finish his rowing career off on a high note. He had been sitting in six-seat up until this point and doing a fine job. He was my natural preference to be moved up to stroke the boat, but as good a job as he was doing in six-seat, he struggled with the responsibility of leading the rest of the crew.

Sterling Reid had been with me for two years as a junior. He was one of those kids who was scary strong. Once, a few years earlier, when I had walked into the school's weight room to workout, a bunch of Grade 8s were in there doing what 13-year-old boys do—competing—and there was Sterling sitting on the squat machine with a couple of hundred pounds of weights and five or six kids on top of that cheering him on as he pushed them up and down the machine's sliders. Given the potential danger to a young growing body, I immediately put a stop to their competition while trying not to show how impressed I was. Now, as a rower, he could generate as much or more power than anyone I had ever coached. At this point in his career, however, he was a little too rough to execute the stroke seat properly.

Given that all of our boats were rigged for a portside stroke, meaning that if you were going to sit in the stroke seat you had to be proficient at rowing with your blade being on your right-hand side, we only had one remaining guy to try out. Like Sterling, Bart-Jan

Caron had been a part of a successful junior program prior to this year. Technically, because of his height, he was quite long in the water and he had decent blade work. Even though BJ, as we knew him, had sat in this seat as a junior and done an excellent job, at the senior level he hadn't quite developed the necessary mental tenacity. Besides, he had enough to deal with. In September he had lost his dad to cancer, and it was everything he could do each day just to show up at practice.

That meant either we changed to a starboard stroke, which I wasn't keen on doing, or we switched one of the starboard rowers over to portside. Given the rigging logistics of changing the boats each day, I chose the latter.

Alex Zorkin, known simply as Zorkin, had been doing a great job in bowseat. Good bowmen are usually the smallest and lightest in size so that they don't make the boat's bow heavy. They also need impeccable technique, and the ability to consistently follow the rhythm of the rest of the crew. Zorkin had rowed for me two years earlier in the junior program as a contributing member to a national championship eight but had taken the previous year off from rowing to try other sports. He was a good runner and a good athlete, skilled at soccer and rugby as well as rowing. Like Jesse, he was smart, but he didn't have Jesse's overt confidence—something he would have to develop. As much as I didn't want to move him out of the bowseat, he was my next obvious choice. When I asked him if he would give it a try, he said yes.

Changing sides is no easy task. It requires taking everything you have learned how to do on one side of the boat and doing it on the other side as a perfectly mirrored image. To make matters worse, Tay, our coxie, wasn't making things any easier for Zorkin. He was so used to Jesse being in the stroke seat that he was finding it hard to accept anyone else being there. Tay was still, perhaps even unconsciously, mourning Jesse's departure. However unfair his tactics, he was ensuring that if Zorkin was going to own that seat for the rest of the season he was going to have to earn it.

After our first week with Zorkin stroking the eight, we were quickly regaining some of the speed we had lost after Christmas. We were back on track and the group's excitement was palpable. Our training seemed to have taken on a new level of intensity, but as much as our workouts were improving, we still hadn't raced anyone with our new lineup. When the under-23 (U23) Canadian national team came up to the school for a weeklong training camp, I saw it as the perfect opportunity to test our speed.

I kept reminding myself that Neil had always raced us against crews that, on paper, should have been a lot faster than we were, and that sometimes we beat those crews. Even when we lost, it often wasn't by much, and the amount that we learned in the process was tremendously worthwhile. We truly had nothing to lose.

Shawnigan's idyllic rowing conditions meant that Rowing Canada held regularly scheduled camps at the school throughout the year. On a Friday afternoon in late February, when I arrived down at the boathouse, I asked the under-23 national team's head coach if it would be okay if we came along for their workout. She said we were more than welcome. When all of my guys arrived, we gathered on the dock and I told them the news. I had decided that it was better to tell them just before they went on the water than to put it in their heads a few days before.

I wish I'd had a camera to catch the expressions when I told them. Some looked quietly excited while others looked scared beyond belief—Travis in particular. Who could blame him? Here he was, a novice rower, about to race the top university athletes in the country—idols of his crewmates. All week long, my guys had seen the national team rowers go by and had stopped to watch them. Now they were going to pull up alongside and challenge them to a race.

We agreed to do a head-of-the-lake piece with a 22 rate cap, meaning that we would race from the top of the lake to the bottom, seven and a half kilometres, side by side, but neither crew could go above 22 strokes per minute. We had done this many times before but never with a crew beside us, not to mention a boatload of under-23 national team athletes.

I gave them their warm-up and shoved them off, reminding them to try and relax and to forget against whom they were racing. I told them to focus on their own boat and not worry about what was going on in the other. With both boats heading up the lake well into their warm-up, I picked up the national team coach on the other dock and we set out to catch up with our crews. When we got to the top of the lake, the national team was already turned and waiting. I told my guys to hurry up and turn the boat around. As the Shawnigan crew finished turning, the national team began rowing. Looking at their faces, I could tell some of them had their noses out of joint about having to race a lowly high school crew. I could fully understand their reaction, but I wasn't about to let this opportunity get away.

"Come on, Tay, get 'em going!" I called out using my electric megaphone.

With that, they sat up and began to row. Within a few strokes, the other coach called out, "In two strokes, begin."

Hold on a second. They're not even?

I thought it, but I wasn't about to say it, given they were doing us a favour. If nothing else, I was about to find out how my young rowers handled starting a piece half a boat down.

It was a calm day, perfect for a long row on this lake. The air was damp and heavy, and the clouds hung low with bundles of white mist dangling seemingly just above our heads. Sound carried easily and quickly across the flat surface of the water. There was no sound like it—eight oars crashing into the water in perfect unison, grabbing a blade full of water and sending the shell surging.

I looked intently for technical issues, checking our rate and comparing our boat speed to that of the more experienced team. As the two boats raced stroke for stroke, I could feel my chest tighten with the anticipation of how this was going to play out. I had suggested this practice and now, in the thick of it, I began to wonder if the experience was going to hurt us or help us?

The national team crew was a big boat and some of them I knew quite well. In fact, sitting in their stroke seat was a graduate of Shawnigan and behind him a Brentwood old boy. They had both left their varsity crew back at Harvard for the week to be here for this camp. As I watched them pounding through the water, I knew that on paper there was no way we stood a chance. We were younger, smaller and less experienced—hell, we had a novice rower in our boat. *What the hell was I thinking?* Three minutes into the piece, neither boat had moved on the other. We were still half a boat down to the national team.

When I looked more closely, my crew still looked scared. It appeared that they were rowing within themselves, not pushing as hard as I had seen them in our own workouts. I turned my coach boat slightly, which brought me in closer to my crew. I pulled my megaphone up to my mouth and said calmly, "I don't know if you noticed. But the other boat hasn't moved away from you. They're just sitting on you. What the hell are you afraid of? Go see what you can do." And with that, I pulled away to see what might happen.

To my amazement, on the next stroke, my Shawnigan crew began to move back on the other boat. The next stroke it was same; stroke after stroke my boat of young teenagers clawed back the lead that the national team crew had started with. We were about 12 minutes into the piece now, just past the halfway point, and what shouldn't have been happening was happening. For another minute or so the two crews sat side by side, exchanging the lead with each stroke.

At first I was obviously thrilled with this turn of events, but then it appeared to me that my crew had stopped pushing again. Stopped striving. That somehow, catching up and sitting even with the other crew was good enough.

I pulled alongside one more time and said, "So that's it? That's as fast as you can go? I don't think so. Dig down and go find out what you're capable of." It was all I could do to not jump out of my boat and climb in there with them. By now, I was getting a little excited.

Once more, on the next stroke, that lowly boatload of high school rowers started to pull away. *Holy shit, would you look at that!* Over the next few minutes, they took one seat after the next until they were leading by open water. I brought the megaphone up to my mouth once again, but this time not to say anything but instead to hide my enormous smile from the other coach.

As we approached the last 1,000 metres of the piece, I could see that the national team had thrown the 22 rate cap out the window. They had cranked their rate and were charging as fast as they could on my crew. There was no way they were going to go down to a high school boat without charging one more time.

Forget that.

I grabbed my megaphone and quickly yelled out, "Okay, Tay, put the whips to 'em! Wind it up, Zorkin! Away you go!" I couldn't help myself. For a moment I was racing again and old habits die hard. When the finish line arrived, my Shawnigan crew was ahead of the national team boat by a quarter of a boat length—a little under a second on the clock. The other coach turned to me with a big smile across her face and said, "Jason, that was a beautiful thing."

As much as it was her job to bring together a successful Canadian crew by the summer, in that moment she too was enjoying a magical moment: nine young athletes having the time of their lives beating a bigger, stronger and much more experienced crew.

I was about to say, "I couldn't agree more," when I heard, travelling across the water, "Three cheers for the U23s! Hip-hip-hooray! Hip-hip-hooray! Hip-hip-hooray!"

Yikes, I wasn't sure how that was going to play out. The three-cheer phenomenon was a West Coast tradition. When I was in high school in the East, there was no way we would have given three cheers for our competition. The sentiment was more, "There, take that, ha!" But there was this young crew, showing what they saw as a sign of respect and a good sportsmanlike gesture. At the end of their cheer, it was returned. Not surprisingly, perhaps, the ex-Shawnigan stroke knew that was the right thing to do. "Three cheers for Shawnigan!"

After a brief rest, we decided to turn and do some shorter pieces, 20- and 30-stroke pieces at higher rates on the way back up the lake. Sure enough, the same thing kept happening: my Shawnigan crew stayed up with the other boat. On the fifth piece, we broke a rigger and had to call it a day.

With the boat put away, I gathered my guys together on the dock. "So how was that?"

They all smiled.

"Awesome!' offered up Big Max.

I grinned. "Okay, I would agree. What made it so good?"

Without any hesitation, Travis of all people spoke up. "Well, when we focused on how we were racing and forgot about who we were racing, we went faster."

Beautiful.

"That's right. I could see it from my coach boat; when you guys stopped worrying about the guys in the boat beside you and started focusing on yourselves in your own boat—you took off."

I looked at all of them one at a time. I could feel their sense of accomplishment, their pride in what they had done that afternoon—it was quite a moment. They had, as a crew, gone well beyond what they believed they were capable of a few hours earlier. I borrowed a line from Neil: "Don't you ever forget this day. Ever!"

Walking home, I was giddy. Most of it stemmed from the enormous sense of relief I was feeling. This approach could work at the senior level—this was our new secret weapon. It was really working: this idea of not focusing on killing our competition was helping us go fast—big time. Tears started to stream down my cheeks as I thought about Travis. I couldn't help myself. I thought about how scared he had looked heading out before the practice. Then, at the halfway point of the race, he and all of the others no longer had any sign of fear in them. Instead, they looked completely calm. Engaged fully in the moment. Executing each stroke the best they could. And loving every second of it.

The next day we talked some more about what had happened against the U23s. We'd all known those guys were faster, but what happened that day provided the perfect teachable moment. I told them I believed the U23s had gone into that practice focused on what they expected to happen—them beating us handily. That expectation meant they were focused on the outcome, not on the process of achieving the outcome.

On the other hand, we had had no expectations of winning. If anything, it would be safe to say that the majority of our rowers had expected to get trounced. Therefore they had had nothing to lose. Not focusing on the outcome enabled them to focus entirely on the process of finding their best race on the day. As they began to achieve it and discover their potential, they connected with the intrinsic satisfaction of just going really fast, and that motivated them to go faster. Conversely, the U23 boat began to struggle when they realized their expected outcome wasn't happening; they became fearful of a different and unacceptable outcome, which made them tighten up and not achieve their potential. It made so much sense.

I also made it clear that although we had outperformed the U23s we were by no means going to be the new national team boat that summer. The crew that we had beat was a throw-together boat, and if they had a week together to properly prepare for a race with us, the results would have, undoubtedly, been drastically different. I made sure my guys were under no illusion that we were now bound for the World Championships. Nevertheless, over the next few weeks, the intensity of our training took another enormous leap. My guess was that the results of our practice with the U23s had generated a sense of tremendous buy-in from all of my athletes. It was a moment when all of us realized that our quest to go as fast as we possibly could and not chase traditional motivators wasn't just about warm and fuzzy idealism but a new strategy that could, ironically, increase our chances of achieving all of those traditional motivators.

At that very moment, things were good. Our perspective was helping us get back on track more quickly. But just when it seemed the sky was the limit, we lost another member of the crew. Pat suffered an injury and would be out for a least a month, so we had to reach into the quad for a replacement. That meant we would be down to 11 rowers. Up until that point we had had enough to boat an eight and a quad. Now, because of the uneven numbers, our training would have to change to accommodate the logistics of having an eight, a double and a single.

Nathan Pocock had just transferred to Shawnigan that year, mainly because the previous senior boys' coach, Andrea Stapff (née Schreiner—my coach from years ago), had encouraged him to. Nathan was an up-and-coming sculler (a rower who rows with an oar in each hand) who felt that attending Shawnigan and being coached by Andrea was a natural step in becoming more accomplished. Unfortunately, the school didn't notify Nathan when Andrea left, so when he showed up he got me, the hammer-and-pull-hard sweep coach.

He seemed to weather the disappointment quite well and easily assimilated into the group. He had spent most of his time in the quad, but as a sweep rower (a rower who rows with one oar in both hands) he had good blade work. Although his erg scores were slightly off the pace compared to the others, putting him in six-seat, where Pat had been, still made the most sense to me, as I didn't want to disrupt the rest of the boat. Toward the end of the term Pat slowly returned to regular training with the rest of the group. He had missed a lot, and his diminished fitness was quite apparent when we did race-paced workouts. It was too much to expect him to jump back in and pick up where he had left off. As much as I was okay with how the boat was doing, we weren't improving at the rate we had been prior to his injury. Somehow, we needed to shake things up.

One night, sitting at my computer at home, an e-mail came in from a young teenage boy named Stephen. He said he was from Calgary and claimed to have pulled an impressive two-kilometre erg test score. *Hmmm.* I sat there re-reading his e-mail looking for signs that it was a joke, that someone had decided it would be funny to present himself as a talented rower looking to come to Shawnigan. I forwarded the e-mail to David Hutchinson, our head of rowing, and asked him whether he thought the e-mail was legitimate or not.

David knew that I needed what this guy had—an impressive erg score. His suggestion was simple—contact him. The next day, I replied to the e-mail, asking for a phone number where he could be reached. To my surprise, he replied immediately. I had to admire his gumption. He was fishing for a new school and was hoping his erg score might land him in my boat. My guess was that Stephen had been checking the results of the Monster Erg Regatta at UVic, where we had competed a few weeks earlier. Big Max had won by over ten seconds and Little Max had finished third. The rest of the crew had raced well enough to make us the top placing high school in the senior boys' division.

With no prohibitive rules limiting athletes from changing schools mid-year, I called Stephen up. He told me that he was going to be in Victoria for a four-day training camp. I asked him if he wanted to come up to the school for an afternoon row, spend the night in a residence and get a real sense of the place. The very next Monday he got dropped off at the school just in time for lunch. By that time I had spoken with his parents. They had been unaware of their son's plans, but after we spoke, they became interested in supporting Stephen any way they could.

As luck would have it, the UVic varsity men's eight had come up to train that afternoon and I asked their coach if we could come out and join them. The plan was to do a number of five-minute pieces at sub-race pace, a hard workout. With everyone gathered at the boathouse, I explained what we would be doing and asked Stephen if he wanted to jump in and try it out. He was hesitant and I couldn't blame him. He was a sculler and had had very little experience rowing in sweeping shells. I told him we would throw him in the middle of the boat where he couldn't mess anything up and that he'd be just fine there. He eventually agreed.

I moved Big Max from starboard side to port and put him into six-seat. Then I put Stephen right behind him in five-seat. I figured Big Max's huge shoulders would inspire Stephen to hang in there.

If ever there was an example of trial by fire, this was it. After a few minutes of getting a feel for it, Stephen was doing okay. Tay was trying to be as encouraging as possible, talking him through each warm-up exercise. Eventually it came time to race. We lined up with UVic and began the first piece. With one minute gone, to my amazement my Shawnigan crew was sitting right beside their varsity boat. On the next piece, they did even better.

After the second piece, I decided to move Pat back into the eight in four-seat to see how he would fare. At first we took off from their varsity crew, but toward the end of the five minutes, Pat was starting to break down, and UVic charged back. He just didn't have the fitness to hang on for the full five minutes. There was still time for him to regain his lost fitness, but given how well the first lineup had gone, and that our races in the spring would be over six minutes, it was going to be a tall order for Pat to knock someone out of that boat.

The next morning, I drove Stephen back to Victoria to meet up with his crew. He told me that he had never done so much work in one practice or gone so fast or had so much fun—he was hooked. Before he left that morning, he wrote the school's entrance exams, scored well and, within a week, was enrolled.

Over the first few weeks, even though he was rough and hadn't trained as hard as we had, having Steve, as we now referred to him, in the boat certainly brought some much needed power and strength, and he was adapting to our technique and our work-load quite well. More than his physical contribution, though, he brought something to our crew that I knew was going to make him an even bigger asset—he had wit, and he knew exactly how and when to use it. That was something you can't learn; you either have it or you don't.

With March came our long-awaited spring break, two weeks away from school and a chance to rest up and recharge before the final push to the end of the year. This year, however, all of my senior guys were going home just for a few days and then returning for an intense 10-day rowing camp of three-a-day rows. It was an opportunity for us to get done in 10 days what would normally take a month. Halfway into the camp, I couldn't have asked for things to be going any better. The guys were working harder than I had seen all year. On the water, they were focused; off the water, they were constantly joking around, and there was tons of inappropriate humour—just the way they liked it. Not only were they getting faster, they were becoming closer as crew. I knew we had hit a good stride.

The camp was also an opportunity for me to see if my new training paradigm could create a chariot full of horses that could effectively compete against more traditionally trained athletes. My plan was to race as much as possible in coxed fours (a four-person shell with a coxswain) and the quad, and break down those old paradigms. I challenged them to help each other find their best performance as a crew. To assist that, I changed the lineup in each boat constantly so they couldn't look at anyone as the enemy to motivate themselves, because the guy they may have tried to beat during one piece was now in their boat for the next. I got them to focus on the things they could affect, like technique, power and how hard they chose to push themselves. It helped create an environment in which the crews that worked together and inspired one another to reach for a better performance were the fastest crews. It worked like a charm.

10 ▶━━━━━━

FALLING OFF THE WAGON

We faced our first big race in April. The Brentwood College International Regatta was important because top crews from up and down the west coast of North America came to compete. Word had gotten out about what had happened at the U23 camp in February. I wouldn't say that we were favoured going into the regatta, but there was certainly some expectation.

We prepared by working on a few more starts without any adjustment to our training. This regatta was important, but it did not warrant tapering off our training. We would push through this one like we would any normal weekend. On the first day, the sun was shining, the wind wasn't too bad and racing times were on schedule. As I made my way over to where the Shawnigan boats were being stored on the field, one of my rowers met me with a mischievous smile. It was James Rogers. He was now our bowman and had rowed for me as a junior two years earlier. He too was in his last year at Shawnigan and was hoping for a memorable end to his rowing career. He was also a bit of a prankster who loved to tease and make jokes. I knew something was up.

"What? What have you done?" For all I knew I would show up to find all of them in girls' underwear and makeup—they were that crazy.

"We have a surprise for you. That's all. Honest," he said with a devilish grin.

When I arrived at the Shawnigan boat trailer, they yelled out "Surprise!" They had rigged our boat. Meaning they had put all of the riggers on the sides, put the seats in and got the boat ready to race. They were so proud of themselves and thought I would be so happy that they had taken the initiative and saved me from doing it myself. There was a slight problem; the reason I always did it by myself was because that's the way I liked it. I wanted to make sure that everything was done just so. It wasn't so much about being a control freak as knowing that everything had been done the way I wanted. If anything went wrong with the equipment, the fault would be mine and no one else's.

Not wanting to seem unappreciative, I bit my tongue and told them that I really loved the gesture. I wasn't about to burst their bubble, so I quietly grabbed my tools and went around the boat double-checking what I could, pretending to be just tinkering.

With everything ready, I called them together. I went over our race plan with them one more time. I made sure that they understood that this was just a chance to check our boat speed against the competition and assess where we were in achieving our ultimate goal in just over a month's time. With that clear, we began the long walk to the dock.

As big as some of my guys were, they were average or even small compared to some of the American crews. The crew noticed it and were worried like I had been years ago at Ridley when all the US competitors were literally heads and shoulders above us. "Look at the size of some of those guys, Dorland!" said one of my boys as we stood waiting to get on the water.

"Tell me how worrying about their size helps you go faster?" I asked.

"It doesn't," he said quietly.

Knowing how much Neil's hand on the back of my neck helped me relax when I was rowing, I squeezed the back of his. "Exactly! They're big, so what? It doesn't change our race plan one bit. Relax, you'll do just fine."

When we got the all clear, we walked down to the dock and got our boat ready to launch. I shoved them off. James, in bowseat, took a stroke to help get the boat out from the dock. As he did that he looked at me and said, "Dorland, there's something wrong with my rigger?"

Then Steve in five-seat spoke up, "There's something wrong with mine as well."

In that moment, I knew what had happened. "Did you check the numbers on the riggers before you put them on?" I asked.

Their looks told me what I wanted to know. "No big deal. Let's go, Tay, get 'em going. You'll be fine."

I knew they were going to be anything but fine. Each rigger is specifically set up for the dimensions of the corresponding width of the shell. You could not choose two seats that were more different in their physical makeup. What had happened was that they'd switched the bowseat rigger with the five-seat rigger, and those two athletes were going to struggle through this race. I had missed it. If I had insisted on re-rigging the boat, I would have caught it, but I hadn't. Furious with myself, I walked up off the dock to watch the race.

Just as I had expected, the starboard side was unable to generate enough power to keep the boat straight. Within the first few hundred metres of the race, my guys had rowed out of their lane and eventually crashed into one of the enormous air-filled buoys that marked the first 500 metres of the race. They stopped rowing, got back into their lane and continued on down the course well behind the leaders. We were not going to qualify for the final. I was as disappointed as they were. Not only weren't we going to the final, we weren't even going to get a chance to test our speed.

Our Ridley College crew after winning the Calder Cleland Trophy in 1983.
Left to right: John Richardson, Steve Garvey, Jason Dorland, Spencer Kraik,
Rob Silk, Tom Wilson, Dave Walker, Kevin O'Brien, Tim Coy. STAN LIPINSKI PHOTO

Gathered at Henley Island after a morning practice a week before we left
for the 1988 Seoul Olympics. *Left to right:* Jamie Schafer, Jason Dorland,
John Wallace, Paul Steele, Kevin Neufeld, Andy Crosby, Don Telfer,
Grant Main, Brian McMahon, Neil Campbell.

Getting ready for our first qualifying heat in Seoul. We had to win this in order to advance to the final without having to race the repechage (second chance). I'm third from the left. COC/THE CANADIAN PRESS PHOTO

During our first race in Seoul. We had a blistering start but couldn't sustain it and finished second to the Russians. The Italian boat is on our right.
COC/THE CANADIAN PRESS PHOTO

Ike and me shortly into his training as a guide dog. He's only 10 weeks old here and had just had a swim at Horseshoe Bay in West Vancouver. When I took him home for Christmas that year, my mom kept asking me how I was ever going to give him back. Luckily, I never had to.

Hearing Robyn Meagher's strategy for this race was the first time I had considered that competition was about more than winning. Here she is looking very relaxed as she runs to a silver medal in the final of the women's 3,000 metres at the 1994 Commonwealth Games in Victoria, BC.

LAWRENCE MCLAGAN PHOTO

A long training session one autumn afternoon on Shawnigan Lake, with Jesse in stroke seat. JASON DORLAND PHOTO

During our 10-day March training camp—breaking down old paradigms around competition—while rowing at Shawnigan Lake School, Vancouver Island. JEFF POCOCK PHOTO

The end of a long day during our March training camp on Shawnigan Lake. JEFF POCOCK PHOTO

Fine-tuning the boat from Hudson Boat Works in St.Catharines, Ontario, days before racing began. With only a few practices to get used to a new chariot, we had to make certain it felt as fast as possible. ROB CARON PHOTO

Max Wyatt and Alex Zorkin having to dig a lot deeper than planned in the coxed four final at the Canadian Secondary Schools Rowing Association (Schoolboy's) Championships in St. Catharines. DIGITAL SPORTS PHOTOGRAPHY PHOTO

The Shawnigan Lake quad— Brad Ingham, Nathan Pocock, James Rogers and Pat Joslyn—sprints to the finish line in the final of their event at the Schoolboy's Championships in St. Catharines. DIGITAL SPORTS PHOTOGRAPHY PHOTO

Just past the halfway point in the final of the eight at the Schoolboy's Championships, the Shawnigan Lake crew is up on the rest of the field by about a half a boat length. DIGITAL SPORTS PHOTOGRAPHY PHOTO

Alex Zorkin, in stroke seat, leads his crew into the last 500 metres of the senior heavy eight final while St. George's beside them refuses to give up.

DIGITAL SPORTS PHOTOGRAPHY PHOTO

Alex Tay, the coxie, calls for everything his crew has left as they begin the final 500 metres of their race.

DIGITAL SPORTS PHOTOGRAPHY PHOTO

The Shawnigan crew pushes to the finish line in the final of the Schoolboy's Championships eight race.

DIGITAL SPORTS PHOTOGRAPHY PHOTO

Winning the coveted Calder Cleland Memorial Trophy. This was the first time that Shawnigan Lake School had ever won a national championship in the senior men's eight race. *Standing (left to right):* Geoff Roth, Sterling Reid, Max Wyatt, Max Lang, BJ Caron, Alex Zorkin, Stephen Connolly, Travis Walsh. *Kneeling:* Shawnigan Lake School Headmaster Dave Robertson and Alex Tay. STAN LAPINSKY PHOTO

My business partner, Ian Walker, and me in front of one of our company trucks, 15 years after founding Skeet & Ike's. It has come a long way since we started making nut spreads at home to sell at the Granville Market in Vancouver.

As much as the eight was our best opportunity to get some solid feedback on how we were progressing, we still had some other races—the quad and the coxed four. I had broken the eight up into two coxed fours, and the quad raced with the lineup that had been training together for the past few weeks. In the end our quad and our top coxed four both finished second in their events behind club crews. Our results suggested we were doing something right; we had to be on track to garner those kinds of results.

With two weeks to regroup and prepare for Shawnigan Lake School's own regatta, I told my rowers and myself to forget about what had happened and refocus. But the next day I ran into James in the main building heading off to class; he was limping.

"What's wrong?"

"I'm not sure. My hip flexor is killing me. It hurts to pull my leg forward to take a step," he said grimacing in pain.

I could tell he was really hurting, but more than that I could tell he was worried. I was worried too. I remembered him mentioning it right after the race but I figured it would have been gone by today. Now, if he couldn't even walk without his leg bothering him, there was no way he was going to be able to row. I sent him off to physio. If James couldn't row, then who was going to sit in his seat? He was doing an excellent job in bowseat, and his two years of racing experience was helping us realize our goal. I only had two more guys that I could use to fill that seat and one of them was a skinny novice rower in Grade 11.

That afternoon when I got to the boathouse, Little Max and Zorkin were also complaining of the same strange pain in their hip flexors. It turned out that our extra-long layback at the finish of the stroke combined with our high-rate work was causing tremendous strain. The quick change in direction at the end of the stroke combined with the fast repetitive action was causing their hip flexors to break down, resulting in severe pain. The answer was rest, stretching and strengthening exercises, all of which we began immediately.

We took that day off, returning to the boathouse 24 hours later to see how everyone was managing. We were now into our last month of preparation; there was no way we could afford any more days off. It was time to get creative.

I decided to switch Little Max to portside and put Big Max back on starboard. The pain didn't seem to bother Little Max when he rowed on his opposite side, but it meant he had only a few weeks to get used to rowing and then racing on portside. Little Max came from an organic sheep farm located in the Interior of British Columbia that his parents had moved to from Germany. He was your stereotypical farm boy—strong and hard-working.

I remember the first year he rowed for me as a junior; we were attending the Monster Erg at UVic and he was warming up for his race. A coach from a rival school came up to me and asked, "What's up with that kid? Nice getup!" referring to his baggy shorts, dark brown socks and old T-shirt that were nothing like the flashy one-piece suits his rowers were wearing. I had to admit, Max looked every bit the country bumpkin. By the end of his race, though, he had not only handily won the junior event but his time had also put him in fourth place in the senior event, not bad for a 14-year-old novice.

As for Zorkin, there was no one else I was willing to switch him with. He was doing an outstanding job in stroke seat and I wanted him to stay there. He said that the stretching was helping and that he felt that he was ready to give rowing a try. Before we could get back to preparing for the Shawnigan Regatta, we still had to find a replacement for James while he recovered from a much worse strain than the others. Brad Ingham had rowed for me a year earlier as a junior. He was the shortest guy on the team, but what he lacked in height he more than made up for with his strength. He also had excellent blade work after spending the majority of the year in the quad. He had a good shot at claiming that final seat.

Besides Travis, Geoff Roth was our one other novice rower. My main concern with Geoff was that he was a lightweight whom I didn't believe had the strength or the stamina to measure up to the other rowers in the eight. I had told them, however, that everyone would have a fair shot at the bowseat and that included Geoff.

We were going to base the selection on what's referred to in rowing as seat racing. There are different forms of seat racing, but I prefer the side-by-side kind, where two boats race over a set distance. After you have recorded the times of the initial race, you switch two rowers—one from one boat into the other boat, and vice versa, and then row back up to the start and race the same distance again and see what changes.

After the first few days of racing, of the three guys challenging for the last seat on starboard, Geoff had come out as the fastest guy, but I wanted one more day to confirm the results and make it crystal clear to everyone who was the best for that last seat. One of the things I disliked about seat racing was that it pitted teammates against one another. Ultimately, selection was an unavoidable part of the sport, but it had the potential to become ugly because athletes raced their hearts out to win the right to sit in a boat. I was pretty sure that the level of respect that existed between these guys was so high that there was no risk of things getting nasty, but I was worried nonetheless. I reminded all of them to focus on the things that would make their own boat go as fast as possible and not resort to trying to kill one another for motivation. I didn't want my last experience in a seat race to be theirs.

In May 1988 at the final selection camp for the eight that would represent Canada in Seoul, I was racing a huge guy from Vancouver for the last seat on starboard side. Neil and I had not been getting along in the weeks leading up to the camp, and I had the sense that he didn't want me in his boat. After losing the first race, I knew that I had to win the second one by well over five seconds to earn my way into the eight. Halfway through the second race my boat was sitting up on my competitor by three seconds. At that point I looked over to the van that was following the race. I could see Neil and the other coaches watching intently.

I remembered an occasion when I was at Ridley and Neil told us that sometimes during a race he would get so mad that he would imagine his competitor's neck wrapped around his oar and the harder he pulled the more it hurt them. In that moment I put Neil's head on the end of my oar and started to pull harder than I ever had. The more I pulled, the more it hurt him and the more incensed I became. By the time we got to the last 500 metres of the race, I had my five seconds and I was going for more. I was determined to make it impossible for Neil to exclude me from his boat. After the race, Neil congratulated me. I shook his hand, looking him in the eye and knowing that he had taught me better than he could have ever imagined.

At the end of the final day of racing, Geoff was the clear choice for bowseat. With one week left to prepare for the Shawnigan Regatta, it was time to get ready to race with our new lineup.

Along with the different free-weight phases that Lloyd Percival had designed for Neil, he had also come up with a number of on-water workouts that Neil adapted to become the backbone of the conditioning regimen for his crews. One of those workouts was 10 by 70 strokes (affectionately known as 70-strokers) at, or above, race pace, which was 38 strokes per minute. Percival's thinking was that 700 strokes was three times the number of strokes that a rower would take during a race. Therefore, if you could survive a practice that involved rowing 700 strokes at a full-out sprint pace, you could survive one race, a third of the workout, more easily. That was the thinking, anyhow.

When Neil first came out with these workouts in the late 1960s and early 1970s, no rowers—let alone high school rowers—were training as intensely as his were. As a result, he dominated the high school rowing scene into the mid-1980s. Given how much that one particular workout had taught me, I had always incorporated it into my coaching. Getting to that day took weeks of preparation and slowly increasing the number of strokes each week until it was time to try 700 of them.

All of the guys in the boat, except for the two novices, had done this workout with me as juniors. They knew how much it hurt, but they also knew how much it would help. The week before the Shawnigan Regatta, it was time to nail it. Before heading out, I reminded them of the importance of what they were attempting that afternoon, that each stroke of each piece was a statement of their trust in each other and that they needed to show up and support one another as they had never done before.

With the warm-up completed, I looked at Tay. He recognized my look to mean one thing—it was time.

He nodded and called for his crew to get ready. "Okay, boys, big breath—here we go."

With that they were off and a few strokes later began the first piece. I throttled up my coach boat and pulled alongside to watch for the slightest imperfection. The whole point of this workout was to do it as perfectly as possible, with no bad strokes. At the end of each 70-stroker I would ask a different rower if that piece had counted—if that one was good enough. If it wasn't, we did it again without a word of complaint. They knew how important it was to get this right. They had heard Neil's words enough times through me: "If you can't do it in practice, you can't do it on race day."

By the time they had six pieces completed, they were well on their way to having the best practice of the year—they were flying. I had never watched a high school crew go after this workout as intensely as they were. They were focused as one crew, together, committed to discovering their physical and emotional limits, then shattering and redefining them with each new stroke.

Neil would always follow us closely during this workout, barking out his commands and trying to help us push our way through each piece, but after the 70th stroke he would move off while we recovered. He gave us two minutes of rest and with approximately 15 seconds left in the break, he would call out over his megaphone that it was time to go again.

That afternoon, I finally realized why Neil kept his distance during the rest. Watching my crew writhe in pain and listening to them gasping for air was something neither he, nor I now, wanted to be held responsible for. Twenty-five years earlier, he had been the reason we pushed ourselves the way we did. He had asked us for our best, and today I was asking the same of my rowers. It was unbearable to listen to them, knowing their pain was my doing. Like Neil before me, I knew all too well how much this hurt.

Even though many coaches had said that Neil's 70-strokers made for an antiquated workout, one based on old science and which no longer served any real training purpose, I begged to differ. I believed that this workout had become more than just a physical test; it was in fact a right of passage for these young men. Just like me in my time, my crew believed that if they could pull themselves through 700 of the hardest strokes and survive, there wasn't anything they couldn't do.

On the last piece, with 40 strokes left, I yelled out for Zorkin to wind it up and called for everyone go with him. I told Tay to drop the ropes (coxies do this to see if the boat is going straight with them no longer steering) and watched the veins in his neck and forehead bulge as he hunched over further into the boat calling out for everyone to empty their tanks. The boat lit up as all eight of them went searching for what it would take to find one last gear. As I watched their blades cut through the water and their bodies heave as one massive unit into the finish of each stroke, tears started streaming down my cheeks. This was truly a beautiful sight—young boys devoted to a cause with such passion and commitment that they would endure whatever it took to ensure they all found success together. The way I saw it, having a boatload of teenagers with that sort of quiet confidence was a powerful place from which to race.

The next day a staff member asked how things were looking for the upcoming weekend. I told him we had had our best row of the year the day before and that I, myself, was excited to see them race. He reminded me that Shawnigan hadn't won the senior boys' eight race at this regatta in years and that a lot of people were hoping this would be our year to win. True to my pledge of nine months earlier, I simply said that we intended to do our best and see what happened.

Later that day I started to think more about what that staff member had told me earlier—that this year presented a good opportunity for us to break the losing streak. The more I thought about it, the more I began to fixate on the notion of winning and being the coach of that winning crew. I began to fall off the proverbial wagon to the point where all I could think about was winning. Without realizing it, I was returning to my old ways of racing to win. Not surprisingly, I also began to revisit my old coaching habits, racing for one reason only—to kill anyone stupid enough to show up beside one of my crews. Deep down inside, despite the façade that I was trying desperately to maintain with my athletes, I was dying to win our upcoming race.

Two days before the regatta, we were out on the course going over our race plan and trying to get used to the buoyed lanes. The lanes weren't completely lined up yet, so Tay was struggling to hold a perfectly straight course. I reminded him a few times that he was continually steering off the line of the buoys and that he needed to pay closer attention to what he was doing. When he veered off the course one more time, I lost it.

"LET 'ER RUN! [Stop rowing!] Tay, what the fuck are you doing? Can't you see that you're not in the same fuckin' lane you were when you started the piece?" I was livid. Tay looked around at where he was and then at me.

"Yeah. I can see that," he answered quietly.

"Then stop writing your name all over the goddamn course. You're going to lose the race for us."

I was out of control. In that fit of rage, I recognized a coach I hadn't seen in years. I steered my boat off the course and drove away, yelling for Tay to do another trip down the course and then take the boat in. I needed to cool down.

As much as I knew that what had just happened was wrong on so many levels, I still couldn't stop thinking about winning—about beating the other coaches. Talking afterward as a crew, I tried to joke around with Tay and lighten the air after what must have been an absolutely shitty experience for him.

With James's hip flexor now relatively pain-free, the quad was busy getting used to its newest member. Although James had sculled a bit before, now he only had three weeks to master rowing with two oars at once and to mesh with his new crewmates. Pat had accepted my decision to move him out of the eight and into the quad. As their new strokeman, he was refocused on helping his new boat find its best performance and was doing an admirable job. James, on the other hand, was still hurting from what he saw as a demotion. I'm sure he understood us having to move forward with the eight healthiest athletes, but he was still upset. I tried to encourage him to see the quad as a new challenge and to understand that his new crew was depending on him.

Saturday, the first day of the regatta, saw the members of the eight race against each other as two coxed fours. The top coxed four finished second behind Victoria City Rowing Club (VCRC). Our second four didn't place in the medals but had a good race nonetheless. As for the quad, despite only having a week to prepare, they came third behind the Gorge Rowing Club and VCRC. Our boat was now undefeated for the season against high school crews and would be heading to St. Catharines as the fastest quad on the West Coast. That performance helped give James a much needed boost of confidence and brought the new lineup closer together.

Sunday was the final for the eight—our last chance to test our boat speed before St. Catharines. Having VCRC in the race offered us the perfect opportunity to test ourselves because they had proven to be the fastest club crew on the West Coast of North America when they'd won the Brentwood Regatta two weeks earlier. They had also won the Opening Day Regatta in Seattle just one weekend before. They were big, strong and fast—it was bound to be a good race.

Robyn had agreed to join me in one of the safety boats that followed along. Having her there meant I would have to be on my best behaviour. I was so worked up by this point that I needed a support system like Robyn to ensure that I didn't say anything stupid. As the boat idled at the starting line, I kept my head down not wanting my guys to see me. I figured they had enough to think about without knowing that I was following along. Normally I just watched from the finish line like everyone else. But given the opportunity to see the entire race, I wanted the chance to spot anything to work on further before St. Catharines.

The start of the race was clean and impressive as all six boats came crashing off the line. There aren't too many sports that rival the intensity, power and thrill of watching the start of an eight race in rowing. With 500 metres gone, we were tied with VCRC and had a three-second lead on the rest of the crews. That lead grew over the next 1,000 metres, but we couldn't shake VCRC, and they couldn't shake us. As we reached the last 500 metres, my heart was pounding and my hands were sweating. I was standing in the boat fighting the urge to yell at my crew. If there was one part of the race that was going to challenge us, I knew it would be the sprint. We hadn't really perfected our rate transitions and, as a result, our final sprint was proving the weakest part of our preparation. Sure enough, with 30 strokes to go, VCRC managed one more rate jump and took a slight lead. Moments later, they crossed the line a second ahead of my crew.

I was furious. They had lost. How could they have done that to me?

"They did well," Robyn said. "I thought they looked good. They have a little more work to do on their finish, though. Aside from that, I'd say they're on track. Congratulations. Way to go, Jase!"

I heard her comments but I didn't believe them. Not one bit. Finish or no finish, they had still lost. Looking over at them as they sat recovering from the race, I noticed that Robyn wasn't the only one who seemed happy with their effort. I could see clearly that none of my guys looked mad or disappointed. *What? Not mad?* They were supposed to be mad—they had just lost. Losing was unacceptable.

I got dropped off at the finish area and went to find my guys who by now had brought their boat up from the lake and were gathered around talking. As I approached them I reminded myself that I had to keep my mouth shut until I was able to cool down. I didn't want a repeat of the other day with Tay.

"Dorland, did you see that?" I bit down hard. *Yeah, I saw that— you lost!*

"That was our best race ever!" said one of the boys.

I couldn't believe my ears. These guys were thrilled with their race. They had come second, lost to VCRC, and they were excited about their performance. That completely threw me for a loop. Even if I hadn't told myself to keep quiet, I wouldn't have known what to say. Their response to losing was beyond anything I had ever experienced or would have ever imagined experiencing. Much to my shock and horror, they continued with their positive affirmations.

"Can you imagine how fast we're going to be in two weeks when we finally nail our sprint? St. Catharines is going to be awesome."

I listened to all of them relive the last 10 minutes with enthusiasm. Then, as if a horse had just come along and kicked me hard in the chest, I was struck with a humbling thought. These young boys, my athletes, had embraced the philosophy that I had set out to teach them better than I had. These teenagers had understood the premise of what we were doing and recognized its potential far better than I had.

At that moment I felt about as small as I possibly could have. My ego had wanted to win—to beat the other coaches. In trying to achieve that, I had lost sight of our goal and what I had been teaching them. In that moment, I had become the student and they the teachers.

Walking to the finish line later that day, Tony Carr called me over to the Brentwood site. "Hey, Jase. Congratulations on your race. Your crew looked good. They say that's the fastest crew VCRC has ever had, and your boys came within one second of beating them. Not bad for little schools like us. Good luck in St. Catharines."

If Tony Carr, one of Canada's most successful high school rowing coaches ever, could see value in the race, then surely I could.

That night I took stock of how far we had come in nine months and how many potentially season-ending challenges we had faced and overcome—all because the perspective we had agreed to adopt was forever there to keep us on track. I finally promised myself, once and for all, that I would not resort to my old ways of motivation, but would join my guys in believing in the process I had started back in September.

Our last week of training before Schoolboy's was, of all things, fun. We continued our taper, ensuring that every workout was packed with quality as the volume of work decreased. We focused hard on our stroke-rate transitions to ensure that our finishing sprint would be the best it could possibly be. I was even able to join in on some joking around and playful banter with my guys. For the moment, the pressure to perform was gone, and I tried as best as I could to enjoy the last week of preparation with these inspiring young men.

Our final day at Shawnigan was spent packing and making sure all of the rowers had enough homework to do during the week that we would be absent from classes. Many of the staff had taken a moment to wish the boys and me "good racing" in St. Catharines, but it was one staff member in particular whose well wishes became the perfect reminder of why I had to stay true to my promise.

While gathering my things in the staff room, he came over to me and said, "Dorland, I don't really care if you win in St. Catharines, as long as you beat Brentwood."

I shook my head and laughed out loud. "Yeah, thanks," I said as I walked out of the room. *How perfect?*

11 ▬▶——————

WHO'D HAVE THUNK?

Early the next morning, I kissed Robyn, Katie and Benson goodbye and made my way to the school to join the others. When I got to the bus, Headmaster Dave Robertson was onboard wishing everyone a safe trip and reminding them that he would be there to see them race on the weekend.

I had brought along the training journal that I had kept during the year. On the plane I passed the time by adding up the total number of kilometres we had rowed during our nine months of training. Not surprisingly, we had rowed about 9,000 kilometres —the equivalent of rowing all of the way across Canada and almost halfway back. I couldn't imagine that any of the crews we'd be racing against would have logged that kind of distance. I figured it was safe to assume that my guys were fit and ready.

The day went smoothly. When you're travelling with 60-odd athletes, half a dozen coaches and a support team of parents, arriving with everyone is a smooth day. We had booked our usual block of townhouse-style residences at Brock University, which is located just outside St. Catharines. The first order of business was to sort out the rooms and unpack. Then, it was off to the Henley course in Port Dalhousie to rig our boats and go for a short row.

That year, with the help of a generous donor, the school decided to purchase a brand new eight for the senior boys. Given that Spracklen had experienced so much success with his World Championship crew in a boat made by Hudson Boat Works, the premier boat builder in Canada, I decided it was good enough for us. We had been told that our new boat wouldn't be ready for this regatta and that instead we would be rowing in a brand new loaner that the national team had just tried out the previous week and had loved. Our boat trailer had set out for St. Catharines four days earlier and had arrived unharmed with all of our racing shells and equipment in perfect condition. When we arrived at the regatta site, two guys from Hudson were there with our racing shell and they couldn't have been more helpful. The boat was beautiful and, more importantly, everyone in the crew thought it would give them an edge. Things were starting to come together.

With everything ready, we carried our beautiful new chariot down for a row. I had been here with almost all of these guys as juniors, but this year was different. The heavyweight eight race was undoubtedly the premier event of the regatta and I was giddy with excitement to watch these young rowers come pounding down the course in a few days.

The crew shoved off from the dock and quickly rowed away to join up with the quad. I had told them to be extra critical of how the boat felt. If something felt out of sorts, I wanted to know. They had one shot at finding their best race on Sunday, and there was no way I would let equipment trouble interfere this time. I walked back up to where the other Shawnigan coaches had gathered and waited to watch my crew come down the course.

The consensus after the first row was that the boat felt great. Big Max wasn't so sure. He thought there was something missing but he couldn't quite put his finger on it. The quad had a good row as well and they were happy with how their boat was coming together. When we arrived back at the university, I told Big Max that we would do some work tomorrow in the eight and maybe that would bring everything together. He seemed okay with that.

Back in my room after dinner, I finally had some time to unpack. There, in the bottom of my suitcase, was an envelope from Robyn—"Open Sunday Morning." I'd known that she wouldn't let this weekend go by without some personal insight and guidance to help keep me grounded. I smiled and put it on my desk. Then I picked it back up and sat down on my bed looking at it and thought about where this letter had begun.

It had all started with that race back in 1994 where she went from second-last to second place. So much had happened since that gorgeous hot summer day in August. If someone standing beside me at that race had told me that I was going to marry the beautiful redhead that had just astounded everyone in the stadium, I would have smiled and said I hoped so. If they had suggested that she would help transform me as a person and a coach so much that I would encourage my future athletes to *not* focus on winning to *improve* their chances of winning, I would have said they were crazy.

The next day, Big Max still wasn't thrilled with how the boat felt. After two rows, some of the others were starting to agree. I had to admit that they didn't look as though they were clicking just right. I remembered what Neil had done with our eight in my last year at Ridley. Instead of having all four of the senior rowers in the front half of the boat and the other less experienced four in the bow, he put me into the bow section with the junior rowers and put one of those juniors in the front of the boat. His thinking was that this strategy helped keep some added length and experience in the back section. It had worked; we had won every race that year.

I had been thinking that maybe we could do the same and move Big Max back into three-seat and Travis up into five-seat. It would give some added length and experience to the bow section of the boat and allow Travis to row up front where there was some added stability. With only two days to go before our race, I couldn't decide if that was enough time for the crew to get used to the change.

Just then, Big Max spoke up. "Jason, what about this idea? Move me back to three-seat and move Travis to five-seat."

I looked at Big Max, smiled and said, "I think you're a genius. Let's do it right now."

It was late and we were supposed to be heading back for dinner, but this was more important. We walked the boat back to the water, made the switch, as well as some small adjustments, and went out for a quick trip of the course.

"Light it up going by the dock, Tay, so I can see how you're running. Okay?"

It had been a long day but if we could end it with a great row, it would set us up nicely for the final few days of our preparation for the weekend. I anxiously watched them go by the dock on the middle part of the course, but they looked solid. When they came into the dock, I didn't even have to ask. Their smiles told me all I needed to know.

I stayed behind with Tay as the others took their oars up to the trailer.

"So, how was that?"

"Jason, they are so ready to race. I can't wait."

"Good. Let them hear that a few times tomorrow during practice. It'll help their confidence."

The next morning I had my two crews go up in behind the island. The water there was always flat and it provided an excellent opportunity to watch them execute a few practice starts. The quad was first. They came off the line beautifully—clean and strong.

"Holy shit! Those guys are fast. James is doing an amazing job!" someone in the eight said.

He was right too. It was just too bad James wasn't able to hear that. I could tell he was still struggling with not being in the eight. Regardless, the rate at which he had gelled with the rest of the quad was impressive.

By now my brother Paul had joined me on the dock to have a look. We stood there anxiously waiting for the eight to do their practice start.

Tay got them ready. "Sit up in all boats. Are you ready? GO!"

Paul and I watched as they came off the line. They were equally as impressive as the quad, hitting 46 strokes per minute. The switch had worked; they were longer at the finish and more controlled going into the catch.

"Jason, if they come out of the gates like that on Sunday, nobody will be sitting beside them. They're fast, all right." Coming from Paul, that was real compliment. He wasn't the type to say something if he didn't truly mean it.

The next day, Friday, saw the coxed four advance quite easily through their first heat; on Saturday, they won their semi-final. The quad also saw their first heat and, like the coxed four earlier in the day, they won easily, with both boats advancing into the final.

The last race of the day was ours, the only qualifying race in the eight. The coxed four, having raced earlier, were warmed up, relaxed and ready to go again. The other four guys, however, would need a good warm-up, not just physically but mentally as well. This was Travis and Geoff's first time at the national championships and, understandably, they were nervous.

"How are you doing, Travis?"

He smiled. I loved that smile—it was so honest. "I'm good. I'm good," he said quickly.

I smiled back. "I'm glad." We both laughed. "You're going to have fun out there this afternoon, okay? You'll be fine—trust me."

He nodded.

Thirty minutes until the start of the race, the call came over the loudspeakers for us to head down to the dock. With the boat in the water, the guys quickly got their blades ready and shoved off. As they secured their feet in their shoes, I said, "Okay, make sure you get a good warm-up and then come down the course the way you know how. I'll see you in a bit. Have fun."

Tay called them ready and they rowed off. Standing there, alone, I felt good—certainly better than in previous years when I had been a nervous wreck. I was really trying to just focus on what I could do as a coach to help my guys and to trust that they would perform as we had prepared to. So far, it was working.

By the time the race started, I was at my usual spot, surrounded by my usual gang—Darb, Davie, Johnny and Kev.

Right on schedule, the race began. Johnny was watching the start with Darby's binoculars. "Hey, Skeet, do you normally row with just seven guys?"

We all laughed. That was exactly what I needed.

"Gimme those." Darb took his binoculars back.

"Jesus, Skeet, they're movin'. They're way up on everyone," Darb said as he squinted to see.

Soon, we didn't need his binoculars to make out the crews. As they crossed the 1,000-metre mark, they were quite far ahead.

"Did you tell them to drop the rate at the 1,000?" asked Darb.

"Yup. I told Tay it was his call. If they had enough lead, they could lengthen out."

Knowing that was what Neil used to tell us when we raced in heats, Darb wasn't surprised.

"What are they at?" asked Davie.

"I've got them at 28 strokes per minute."

"Christ, they're still moving away," added Johnny.

As they went by us with 500 metres to go, I looked hard to see if there was anything that I could mention later for them to improve for the final, but I had to admit, they looked good.

The gun sounded as they crossed the line. We had qualified for the final—our last hurdle. They announced our time as being six minutes and two seconds. *Whoah, 6:02 at 28 strokes a minute for half the race into a headwind—I'll take that.*

"They looked good, Skeet. Should be a good final tomorrow," said Davie.

It was certainly looking that way. Although we had the fastest qualifying time, the other two heats had posted good times as well, and their winners hadn't necessarily been pushed either. It was time to go home and rest up for tomorrow. First I went down to meet my guys.

When they came into the dock they were all business. "What's wrong, Tay?"

"Nothing," he said quickly.

"How'd that go?"

"Good. They were really strong off the start. We were clear of everyone in 30 strokes. I kept the rate up because I wanted to get a 1,000 metres in for the guys who didn't already race today." Tay was still quite serious given how well things had gone. "Then when we lengthened out to 28, it was the strongest low and hard we've ever done. It was so solid."

"That's good. That was a good call," I assured him. "And, yeah, even Darb and the gang commented on how strong you guys looked. But why does everyone seem so mad?"

"I don't know. I guess they're getting ready for tomorrow. Coming back to the dock, I told them that today was good, but we had to refocus on what was coming tomorrow."

The van ride back to Brock was quiet. Something was up. Sure, they were focused, but this was beyond that—something had happened.

As they were heading off to their rooms to get showered up, I called Travis back.

"How was that, Travis?"

He grinned. "That was so much fun, Dorland," he said almost apologetically. "I've finally figured out why we trained so hard all year."

"Why's that?" I asked.

"That was so intense. We were flying out there," he answered with boyish charm.

I laughed. "You think that was fun. Just wait until six o'clock tomorrow evening—now that's going to be fun."

He laughed and ran off to his room. As I turned to go to mine, my phone rang. It was Scott, my oldest brother. He was phoning to congratulate me on the win and to ask me why my guys had kept their blades up for so long at the end of the race.

"What do you mean?"

"At the end of the race, they balanced the boat with their blades up."

"Yeah? I don't know, it's just a discipline thing, I guess. The same way we did with Neil. Why?"

"Jason, they balanced their boat for 40 seconds, until the last crew crossed the line."

"They did what? Thanks, Scott. I'll call you later."

I walked straight into Tay's room. "What's this about balancing with the blades up until the last crew finished?"

He looked down. "I don't know what happened. We crossed the line. We took three strokes and then I called for them to let it run. Their blades went up like usual, but then just when I was about to call them down, someone yelled out to leave them up. The other guys started yelling to put the blades down, but then the guy who said to leave them up yelled back to keep them up. There was more yelling and then, finally, when the last crew crossed the line, we put them down. I think that these guys are so disciplined, no one would break rank and put his blade down on their own. Zorkin was so mad."

"Who was it yelling to keep them up?" I asked.

"Big Max," Tay answered quietly.

"Shit, Tay, that's not what we're about. You know that!" I was furious.

"I know, but the worst part is that when we rowed past the grandstand on our way back to the island, we got booed."

"Go get everyone, right now. I don't care what they're doing. We need to sort this out."

I went into the living area of Tay's apartment and waited. When everyone was there, I asked what had happened. Tay's version was consistent with the others, including the part about Zorkin being furious. He wasn't the only one. All of them were pissed about what had transpired after the race. Big Max was getting an earful from his crewmates. I didn't need to speak up. He knew that what he'd done wasn't smart, and by the time we had finished clearing the air, he felt badly about it.

On one hand I could understand his sentiment. He was the only returning member of the Shawnigan senior crew from last year. It had been a frustrating year for him, culminating with a third-place finish in the final. This year, he felt vindicated in telling all of the other schools that he was back with a crew that was considerably faster and more committed. None of that made it right.

"You realize that what you guys did will spread quickly, and if you think you had a target on your backs before the race, you can't imagine how big it is now. The crews you'll be racing tomorrow don't think like we do. They all want to kick the shit out of you. Even more so now, and I can't blame them; that was arrogant, unsportsmanlike, rude, you name it. It's not about sticking it in the face of everyone else. We race for each other—that's it. That's all you have to worry about. Are we good here? Is everybody okay?"

It appeared as though everyone had said what they wanted to say and they were ready to move on. I sent them back to their rooms satisfied that our team was still a team despite a potentially disastrous incident. If Scott hadn't phoned to tell me about their stunt, and we had gone back to race the next day with the amount of animosity that was still in the crew, it would have undoubtedly affected their ability to perform.

Once again, the credence of Robyn's approach was apparent. Imagine if we had done that and meant it? What a horrible way to alienate yourselves from your competitors. Going down there with a humiliate-your-competitors approach to racing, we had almost self-destructed as a crew. It was, yet again, a great lesson for every-one—me included.

Later that night I slowly made my way from room to room, saying goodnight to each of my guys. They were now much more relaxed; they'd moved on from what had almost torn us apart earlier in the day. In a word, they were excited. With our Henley Royal Regatta trip having been cancelled a few weeks earlier due to finan-cial reasons, we all knew tomorrow was it—their last chance to show themselves and each other how hard they were willing to race to find the best performance of their lives.

No one summed it up better than Pat. By now, he had more than accepted that he was a member of the quad; he had embraced it and made the stroke seat his own. When I walked into his room, he and his roommate, Nathan, were lying in their beds talking.

"How are you guys doing?" I asked.

"Good, Dorland. I'm ready to go," answered Nathan.

"Glad to hear it. How about you, Pat?"

"I'm good, too. I've been thinking, though. Tomorrow is my last rowing race, ever. I've been doing this since Grade 8 and tomorrow it's over. I've told myself that to leave this sport on my terms, I have to have the best race of my career. I've made a deal that if I can row harder than I've ever done before and tell myself that there was no way I could have gone harder at the end, then I'll be happy with my race no matter how we do."

"Pat, I can't imagine a better way to go into your race. Just go out there and race as hard as you can and have fun doing it. It's that simple." I walked to the door and turned off the lights. "Have a good sleep, boys."

When I woke up the next morning, the first thing I did was read Robyn's letter.

Good morning Jason,

I hope your final week of preparation has proven a good one. I wanted to take this opportunity to tell you how proud I am of what you have accomplished on a personal level and as a coach in the last nine months. You have grown far beyond who you once were and have taught your athletes more than just how to row and race well. You have shown them how to be good competitors and good people. Know that the results of today's racing will in no way define your impact on your crew. Whether you win or lose, you have won.

Be your best. Love, Robyn

Okay, that's not fair, Robyn!

This wasn't good—streaming tears and I was only minutes into the day. I donned my sweats and took off for my morning run, my last chance to clear my head and prepare for the biggest day of the year. As much as I knew Robyn was right about the outcome not defining our year, I also knew it was my job to do everything in my power to ensure that my boys found their best races today. Running along the trails near Brock, I thought about Neil and what he would have been doing the morning of the finals when I was racing for him. What were his rituals, if any?

Despite Neil's size and tough outer persona, he was a tremendously sensitive and caring man who loved on a deep level. He loved his wife, his daughters and his dogs. He loved his rowers as well. He lived and died with them through their triumphs and failures. He was the epitome of an athlete's coach—connected to them through more than just circumstance. At that moment I longed for that connection one more time—his big warm hand squeezing the back of my neck.

Thinking of Neil brought the names of old Ridley rowers flooding back to me—young teenagers, not unlike my rowers, who had also dreamt of racing the waters of Martindale Pond faster than they ever had before. I began to think that, in some way, what happened during the races later that day would be somehow a reflection of Neil and all that he represented. If I was successful, then somehow Neil was as well. The weight of that comparison and the responsibility it held was too much. I tried to lose that thought immediately.

The other part of Robyn's letter that I thought of was the whole "being proud of me" part. I had always struggled with the idea of making people proud of me. What young teenager didn't strive for his parents' recognition and approval? I was no different; hearing "I'm proud of you, Son" was undeniably one of the main reasons I participated in sport.

I remembered the final day of selection for the eight that would row in Seoul. By the time I got home that afternoon, Mom and Dad were at a dinner party over at Ridley. Paul had dropped them off earlier and, when I got home from my racing, I told my brother that I would drive over and pick them up. When I arrived they were walking out of the main entrance of the school and heading toward me as I stood by the car. I could tell by the look on their faces that they were excited to hear the news but also worried about what that news might be.

"How did it go?" asked my mom.

"Mom, Dad, I'm going to the Olympics."

They both cheered—they were overjoyed. I had never seen them so excited about anything that I had accomplished in my life. Mom gave me huge hug while Dad gave me his trademark firm handshake, but what rang out loud and clear, above all of the things they said, was that they were both proud of me. I knew they had undoubtedly told me that many times before, but I had never heard, never felt it, like I did in that moment. Remembering that moment on my run all these years later, I yearned for those words again.

My relationship with compliments was a strange dichotomy. On one hand, I sought praise from my parents; on the other hand, as a young teenager I had convinced myself that compliments were dangerous. That if I heard them, embraced them, savoured and enjoyed them, I would begin to believe them. At which point I would become complacent and weak, thereby diluting my drive to train and be the best. When I heard praise, I simply tuned it out. After years of playing that ridiculous game, I was hearing Robyn's words and finally feeling their sentiment. Robyn was one of few people whose opinion truly mattered, and that she had recognized my growth and efforts over the past decade meant something dear to me. That allowed me to end the run in a good space—I was ready to enjoy the day.

By the time we arrived at the course for the coxed four final, I could feel my tension and anxiety about the outcome of today's races creeping back. My brief escape from the pressures of the day was short-lived and I was back to reality. I tried tinkering with our boat, rechecking everything, desperately seeking the relaxed state I had enjoyed on my run. Amid the commotion of boats and crews coming and going, I noticed a huge shadow beside me. It was Darb. Good ole Darby—so dependable, so supportive. I couldn't begin to count the number of times that he had been there to help me out before, and here he was, one more time, showing up to say in his quiet way, "I care and if there's anything I can do to help, just ask."

"How you doing, Skeet?" he asked with a warm smile.

"Shitty!" I paused for few moments while Darby waited patiently for me to continue. "Darb, I gotta tell ya. I know it sounds crazy, but I can feel the weight of every guy who ever rowed for Neil on my shoulders right now. And if we lose today, then I will have somehow let them down."

"Don't be so stupid, Skeet. You've done everything you can do to get your guys ready for today; they're good to go. Stop worrying about it, okay? I'll be over on the bank if you need help with anything."

Darby was right; this was not the time to worry about anything other than my crews. In her letter, Robyn had referred to engaging in the process of the journey and enjoying it. That's what I needed to remember. That's what would keep me grounded and on track, not worrying about whether or not I was living up to someone else's expectation.

With one hour before the four race, we met at our boat. They all looked good—fresh and ready to go.

"Okay, we're into less than 60 minutes before our race. You have 20 to go to the bathroom or fill up your water bottles or whatever else you need to do. Otherwise stay out of the sun and I'll see you here in a bit. Okay?"

After the four rowers had walked away, Tay spoke up. "Jason, you need to relax. I can feel your tension and I'm sure the boys can too. It's not going to help them."

Wow! That took some gumption. "That bad, eh?"

Tay nodded. "That bad."

"Can you stand by the boat? I'll be back in a second." It was time for a short walk.

Listen, Jase, you're their coach. It's your job to identify all of the tasks that you can take care of today that will help these guys race to their potential. Being nervous is not one of them. Smarten up and start helping.

I walked around for a few moments longer, just to move, breathe deeply and settle down. With that done, I returned to Tay and the boat. I felt a lot better and I was finally ready to get on with some good racing.

"Tay—thanks. I don't imagine that was easy. I appreciate it, though. I'm all good now—don't worry."

Right on time, with 30 minutes to go before the final, we were walking down to the dock. With everyone ready, they shoved off and made their way up to the starting line. I watched for a while from the dock before heading off to join the rest of the gang.

"Hey, Skeet, how are they doing?" asked Johnny.

"Good."

There wasn't much else to say. My four guys had only had a few weeks to sort out their new lineup, but given that they had raced well at our regatta, I was expecting the same today. The only reason I had even agreed to enter this race was because of how fast they were and how experienced each rower was. With only four hours to recover before the eight final, it was a gamble, but one I'd felt safe making given their speed and fitness.

"Jesus, Skeet. It's close. I don't even think they're out front," Darby said as he strained through his binoculars to get a better look.

With that news, my heart sank. *What had happened? Something had definitely gone wrong. These guys were just too damn fast for it to be close at this point in the race.*

By the 1,000-metre mark, they had moved out in front of the other crews. As they went by us at the 1,500, they were pulling away comfortably, but it was still closer than it should have been, and they were working far harder than I would have wanted. I relaxed a bit at the sound of the gun, but I was still shaken given how close it had been.

Had we missed our taper? Were the other crews playing with us that much during the heats?

.   These questions continued as I left the gang and made my way down to the dock to meet them as they came back. Along the way, a few coaches congratulated me, but I wasn't celebrating anything. By the time the crew made their way into the dock, I was there to meet them. I was so focused on finding out what had happened that I didn't even take the time to congratulate them. When I asked how they'd done, Big Max smiled and shook his head.

"Sorry, Dorland," said an embarrassed Little Max. "I caught a boat-stopper and then we had to come back—a lot."

"Yeah, but we did, and that's the main thing," added a tired but satisfied Zorkin.

After we had brought the blades and the boat up to the stretchers, we gathered around quickly to sort out the details. Still obviously wound up from the race, Tay started, "Little Max caught a huge crab about three strokes into the race, which stopped the boat and turned it on about a 45-degree angle. We straightened out the boat and got going again. By then the other crews were gone. Some of them had to be two or more boat lengths ahead. I was thinking it was going to take some serious racing to come back from that far down."

Then Big Max spoke up. "It was all good. Everyone kept their cool and we just put our heads down and started laying down some serious strokes," he said with a contented smile.

They were tired; it was obvious they had gone much harder than we had planned for.

"How about you, Little Max? How are you doing?" I asked looking at him.

"Okay," he replied.

"What happened? Did something break? Or did you just catch a crab?" I asked.

"I don't know. I think I just might have had a bad stroke. I'm still not all that comfortable on portside and once in awhile I lose it. I didn't hear anything break when it happened, though. I just knew that when we were straight again, it was time to pull—really hard," he finished, obviously relieved and exhausted.

With everyone having offered all they had to say, I gestured for Tay to move away so we could speak.

"How are they doing?" I asked him.

"Jason, I've never felt them go that hard before. It was impressive the way they came back and just mowed everyone down. They didn't get rattled at all. It was like we were back on the lake at home doing pieces against each other—it was great. I loved it. I'm so proud of these guys."

"Okay, okay. Now we've got to rest them up for the eight. Make sure they have a light snack with plenty to drink. Keep them out of the sun and don't let them nap. One of the parents is going to shuttle you back to Brock and then bring you back here in time for the eight. Understand?"

Tay was beginning to calm down after what had to have been a real test for him. A good deal of the credit for salvaging that race would have to go to him for having the presence of mind to simply and calmly assess the situation, and then talk the guys back into the race. He had done a great job, but it was time to refocus on the real reason he had come here.

Next up for me was the quad. By then, I felt almost giddy. What had just happened had thrown me into a place where I had to acknowledge that this was a race day, when anything and everything could happen. I had no choice but to focus on what I could affect—the mental readiness of my guys and nothing else.

Earlier that morning at Brock I had done our race visualization with the quad and the four, so there was nothing to sort out in terms of race strategies—they knew exactly what to do. Now Pat was all smiles; I had never seen him so relaxed. Even a reluctant James had been caught up in the excitement of preparing for this race over the past few days and was keen to get going, as were the other two, Nathan and Brad.

Standing on the dock before they shoved off, I asked Pat if he was ready.

"Well, I've got nothing to lose, Dorland. And just like I said last night, I'm going to race harder than I've ever done before today, and if I can do that—I'll be happy." With that, they shoved off.

I knew that it was going to be a tough race. We were the fastest crew from the west, but we hadn't raced the two top crews from Ontario, and the times in the heats had been within seconds of each other. It would take a perfect race to come out on top.

As they went by me with 500 metres to go, E.L. Crossley was out front with a slight lead, while Ridley and Shawnigan exchanged second place with each stroke. It didn't get much more exciting than this. Minutes later the first gunshot sounded followed closely by two gunshots one after the other. E.L. Crossley had won and Shawnigan had come third to Ridley.

I met my guys at the dock, where Pat announced, "That's the best race I've ever had—I've never gone that hard before," obviously proud of his accomplishment.

"That's all you can ask, Pat. Good for you! Congratulations!"

I was so excited for these guys. They had been the spare boat for the eight the entire year, and their lineup had changed many times in the past nine months. Here they were at the end of their season racing the best they could on the day, and being happy and satisfied with it. As a coach, how could I find fault in that? Sure, they hadn't won, but on the day when crews are that close in ability it's truly anybody's race.

By then, I was having a better day. In fact, I had never been so relaxed at a regatta, ever, but when the coxed four showed up and Little

Max told me that he was still feeling spent from the four race and wasn't sure if had he enough juice to go again, I started to panic.

Beautiful, Jase! This is great. The one race you've been training these guys for all year and you've just compromised it with the coxed four race. Way to go, buddy!

Remembering what Tay had said to me earlier, I knew I couldn't let these guys know how much I was freaking out.

Breathe, Jase. Calm down. Look, there's only one thing to do here—focus on what your guys need and then be their coach.

When the remaining four arrived, they looked rested and excited but anxious to get the race started. They had been back at Brock on their own all day—it was now five o'clock—and they were bursting and ready to race. With less than an hour to go, I knew that these four guys were going to make or break our performance.

As Sterling made his way back from the washroom to where the others were gathered, I stopped him. "You ready to go?"

"Like never before."

"Good, because the coxed four is tired. Their race took more out them than we had anticipated. So I need you to step up like you've never done before. Can you do that, Sterling?" I asked, looking right into his eyes for any sign of fear.

He smiled, and I realized there was none—not even a speck.

I felt a funny sense of calm come over me as I took Geoff, Bart and Travis aside one at a time and told them what was up. They needed to know how much their teammates were relying on them. Each of them, one after the next, smiled and said they were ready. It was as if they felt more excited for the added challenge. In some way they had played second fiddle to the top four all year long and now it was their turn to shine. I took comfort in their confidence.

John "Munch" McIntyre, a crewmate of Neil's from the national team and good friend, had made arrangements to drive Neil onto the compound in front of the boathouse that faced the racecourse so that he could watch the final for the eight. Neil and Munch were like royalty on Henley Island. I watched as people came up to his window to say hello. Neil was now suffering from full-blown Parkinson's and was rarely seen in public; therefore many of the coaches took time to pay him a short visit.

The debilitating disease that was now causing him so much frustration and discomfort had apparently been impairing his thought processes and decision-making in 1988. It explained so much of the anger and irrational behaviour that he had heaped on me back then. Knowing that now allowed me to let go of so much of the anger I held around my relationship with him, so when there was an opportunity, I walked over to say hello. Because his speech was limited, I wasn't sure if he would be comfortable meeting my guys. He was an extremely proud man and sometimes wasn't keen on people seeing him in this condition. He managed an audible yes and gestured for me to bring them over.

When they had all gathered, I said, "I'd like you to meet Neil. He's over in that truck." I pointed at the black truck that was parked 30 metres away. "Just so you know, he has trouble speaking, and he can't sit still but he wants to meet all of you. Introduce yourselves and tell him whatever you'd like. It's best if you guys lead the conversation. If he does say anything, you'll have to get in close to hear him. Okay?"

We walked over to the truck. "Neil, these are my guys."

With that I stepped back and let them get in close to introduce themselves. Standing a few feet away, I could hear that Neil was speaking. This was great. Here was Neil, my high school coach, talking to my crew moments before they went out to race the same event that he had coached me in 20 years earlier. I felt good, and I could feel Neil's excitement from where I was standing. The "coach" was still in him. The posture of my guys told me they understood the significance of whom they were meeting and what it meant to me.

As all nine of them leaned into the truck to hear this rowing legend share some last-minute words of encouragement, I was remembering what it was like to have Neil as a coach in high school. He wasn't much for pre-race talks, but his look, his few perfectly selected words, his very presence could make you want to race harder than you ever had before. He knew he had prepared you and that all there was left to do was race. That was a feeling that I loved as an athlete—that all of the work was done and it was now just about racing.

After my crew had said their goodbyes to Neil, I went over to him to say thanks and tell him that I would see him after the race—he was all smiles. I caught up to Big Max and asked, "What did he say?"

"It was sort of hard to understand, but at the end he said, 'Pull. Just pull hard.' Perfect. How perfect is that? If you think about it, that's really what this last race is going to come down to. Pulling!"

"Great. I'm glad you guys got to meet him. He's quite a man."

Big Max smiled.

Ten minutes before our race would be called, I gestured for everyone to come in. "Okay. How's everybody doing? Good?"

They all nodded.

"Great. Because in just half an hour, if we're going to find our best race ever, we're going to need the best we can get from each one of you. You know our race plan. You know what you have to do to achieve that. Remember more than anything else, if we go out there looking for our best performance, it'll show up. I promise. And if you get tired and you want some help, I'm right there with you every stroke—believe me."

As the speakers crackled to announce our race, we were already walking down to meet the boating officials. With each guy accounted for, we were given the okay to head to the dock.

"Good luck, Shawnigan," offered an official. I smiled to acknowledge his gesture.

As they stood waiting to get in the boat, I made my way through the crew one last time shaking their hands and wishing them well. When I got to Bart, he took off his necklace, which had a ring hanging on it, and passed it to me.

"Can you keep this for me, Dorland?" he asked. "It's my dad's ring."

"Of course I will." I took the ring in my hand. "You know he'll be right there with you all the way down."

That was as much as I could offer—I had managed to keep my emotions in check so far and I knew that talking about Bart's dad would choke me up for sure. I wasn't going to lose it now; I just squeezed his neck and smiled.

Finally, when I got to Zorkin, he was standing ready to shove off.

"You're the perfect guy for this job. Just do what you did earlier today and you'll be fine. You've got seven guys ready to back you up as much they can. Take them as far as you want to go. Okay?" He nodded. "Have fun with it."

With Tay sitting ready in the boat, I squatted down to have a final word with him. "Okay, Tay. Everything ready?"

"Yup, we're good."

"Even though the four is tired, do the regular warm-up. Push the rates on the starts. It'll build their confidence and get them excited. Otherwise, straight down your lane. And when it's time to go, get out your whip and squeeze everything you can out of them. They'll respond. Okay?" He nodded. "Have fun. We'll see ya back here in a bit."

Tay spoke up, "Okay, boys, this is it. Here we go. Everybody one foot in. Ready? Shove."

I grabbed a blade and helped move them away from the dock. They quickly strapped themselves into their shoes and began their final row together up to the starting gates.

I made my way down to my usual perch where my support group was waiting.

"All ready, Skeet?"

"As ready as we're gonna be, Darb." The tension was starting to get to me and it was showing.

"Don't worry, Skeet," Johnny said. "As long as they win, everything will be fine. If they don't, it'll all land on your shoulders." Everyone laughed at his attempt to break the tension.

Despite the fact that he was kidding and that I had told my crew that the outcome of this race, whether we won or lost, was not what we were going to focus on, I knew that all of our time and effort would be judged worthwhile or not in the next few minutes.

With Darby closely watching the starting gates through his binoculars, we all stood there quietly waiting.

"They're off!"

Silence. We all held our breath waiting for Darb to tell us how they had come out of the start.

"Everyone is away clean. Your guys look good. I think they're up already. It's tight though. It's hard to tell. But they look as though they have a slight lead."

Still, no one else was saying anything. Even Johnny knew that from here on he was better off holding his otherwise witty comments for another time. We all just stood watching in one direction, waiting. A few moments later we could make out the crews as they came through the first 500 metres. Traditionally, this is where teams would start to initiate power strokes or surges in boat speed in an attempt to break away from their competitors.

By now the announcer was calling Shawnigan with a lead of half a boat length (about one and a half seconds), with St. George's from Vancouver in second, followed immediately by a tightly packed field. At the halfway mark, we were still up, but it was close. Although I would have much preferred a strong headwind to sort out the fitness levels of each crew early on in the race, the day's tailwind would be helpful for my tired crew. Coming by our vantage point, Shawnigan still held onto a slight lead, but St. George's and E.L. Crossley were sitting second and third—comfortably within striking distance for the final sprint.

Now I was panicking. The crew's fatigue was showing up in spades. Twenty-four hours earlier, we had easily won our heat by 12 seconds. Now we were barely holding onto a one-second lead going into the last 500 metres.

Come on, boys. Dig in. Dig in. Time to go, Tay. Now—drop the hammer, buddy!

"They gotta go, Skeet! It's now or never."

As a stroke man for almost his entire rowing career, Darb knew more than anyone that when you came into the last 50 strokes of the race, every one of them mattered.

"There they go!" said Johnny. "Holy shit, they just jumped a few strokes [increased their stroke rate]."

They had, too. You could see the shift in their rate. They were going after this final sprint with every last bit of strength they could muster. But St. George's was still right there with them. They were not about to quit. Not with less than a minute to go. It was evident that my crew would need to call on the best sprint of their lives to hold them off.

I wanted to yell, scream something. No one word in particular—just something to release all of the energy that was now pent up inside of me. I now knew why Neil watched us race alone—this was torture.

Darby, facing the finish line, squinting through his binoculars, waited to see who would cross first.

"They got 'em. I think they got 'em. They're flying. They gotta be pushing 44 at least."

BANG!

Followed closely by another BANG!

"You got 'em! Your guys came down before St. George's. I'm sure you won it, Skeet." Darb was about as excited as he got.

I still wanted to hear it officially. I wasn't about to take anything for granted at this point.

"Did you see them jump as they started their sprint? There's no way St. George's could hold onto that kind of a sprint." John was trying to reassure me that it was a done deal.

Soon after, like a judge reading my verdict, the announcement came over the loud speakers. "The results from event number 36, the final of the senior boys' heavy eight. First, Shawnigan."

Exhale. One simple and glorious exhale. *Holy crap, did that feel good.* They had done it. Despite the challenging day we had experienced, they'd still managed to hang on and pull off the race of their lives.

"Second, St. George's. Third, E.L. Crossley. Fourth, Kingston. Fifth, Vancouver College. Sixth, St. Mary's. The winning time, 5 minutes and 47 seconds." *5:47? That was fast.* For a high school crew to break six minutes over 2,000 metres was one thing, but going 5:47 was something altogether different—that was an amazing time.

After accepting congratulations from the gang, I walked off to be alone. I just needed some time to breathe—to digest this moment. It had been a long day, a long year filled with moments where I thought we would never arrive at this day as one complete crew. And yet here they were—they had truly arrived. Walking off on my own, I could easily picture in my mind what was happening to my crew at the grandstand. The image made me smile. Both for the memories of my experience and now the satisfaction that I had helped these young boys arrive at a place where they were now living exactly what I had 20 years earlier.

After the fourth-, fifth- and sixth-place crews had cleared the finish area, my crew, along with St. George's and E.L. Crossly, would be called into the grandstand, where they would all stand as individual crews on the medal podium. After the silver and bronze medals had been awarded, my Shawnigan crew would have their gold medals placed around their necks one at a time by the presenting official. Our headmaster would join them on the podium to congratulate each of them and then, finally, the Calder Cleland Memorial Trophy, the most expensive trophy in all of Canada, would be presented to them. At that moment they would hoist it in the air while parents, teammates and other Shawnigan supporters in the crowd cheered in appreciation of their accomplishment. Then they would be asked to gather around the enormous gold and silver cup and pose for a picture to commemorate their having captured the title of Canadian National Champions. Finally, as is customary in rowing, they would pick up Tay and carry him over to the edge of the dock and begin to swing him back and forth to the encouraging countdown of the crowd. On the third and final swing, they would release him into the air. He would scream in celebration before splashing down into the waters of Martindale Pond. It was a scene that replayed itself every year on this weekend, a scene that my guys would own for the rest of their lives. For me, that felt good.

As I walked back to the dock to meet my crew, I could see that Neil and Munch hadn't left. I veered over to say goodbye.

He turned to see me. "Jase. They did it." His speech was excited and clear.

"Yeah, they managed to hold on, Neil."

"Congratulations. They looked good."

Munch stuck his hand out. "Yeah, way to go, Jase. Congratulations! They looked like a strong crew out there."

"Thanks, Munch. Thanks, Neil." I was feeling a bit overwhelmed by now. Being congratulated by two men, two coaches the calibre of these two, wasn't something that happened every day. What my Shawnigan eight had just accomplished was beginning to sink in.

Ever the coach, Neil piped up one more time. "That's one hell of a layback your guys had. What was that for?" I laughed and explained what we had been trying to do. "Well, it worked, whatever you did," replied Neil.

With that I could see my guys coming into the dock. "I'm just going to grab my crew. Are you leaving right away?"

"Pretty soon," answered Munch. "I told Mary I'd have Neil home for dinner." Neil laughed.

"Can you just hang on for one minute? I'll be right back." I ran down to the dock. It was quiet now. No crews were around. It was just the dock official and me. He offered his congratulations as I approached and told me the dock was mine to bring them in anywhere I wanted. With that he left me on my own to wait. I signalled for Tay to slow it down just a little. With the adrenalin pumping, it was easy for crews to come into the dock far too quickly and take off their bow section. I knew that first-hand.

With one last stroke, they were balanced and landed perfectly. I grabbed a blade and brought them to a final stop. I wasn't sure what to expect. Would they be hyper? Giddy? Serious? They were none of those. They were quiet. But they had these big grins. It was kind of a "Well, we did it—now what?" grin.

"So how fun was that?" I asked.

"That was awesome."

"I'm glad. I'm glad you had so much fun out there. I'll bet that was one hell of a race." They were quiet again. "Now, you have to know how proud I am of all of you for what you guys accomplished here today, and over the past nine months. But before you get out of the boat, I want you to do me a favour. I want you to row back up to the gates again and then come into your lane one more time. But this time, I want you to row in complete silence. Tay, turn off your speakers. While you're rowing I want you to think about three things. I want you to think about all of the challenges that you have faced this year as individuals and as a crew. Then I want you to think about all of the lessons that you've learned as a result of those challenges. And, finally, I want you to reflect on what each and every one of you means to each other in that boat. When you're done that, come on in. Okay?"

Without prompting, Tay took over. "One hand on the dock. Ready to shove? Shove."

I took hold of Travis's blade and helped push them out. "I'll be here when you get back. See you in a bit."

They rowed away in silence with only the sound of their oars grabbing and releasing the water as they made their way up the course one last time.

Each winning crew was awarded two plaques while on the podium, a large one for the school and a smaller one for the coach. Before the guys left, I grabbed my coach's plaque from Tay and then ran back up to the truck where Neil and Munch were still waiting.

Reaching into my pouch with all of my tools, I found a marker. I pulled it out and began to write on the back of the plaque.

Neil, Thanks for all of the lessons you taught me.
Love always, Jason.

"Neil, I want you to have this," I said, offering the plaque. "They did what they did today because of what you taught me. You're the reason they were so fast." I paused as I started to choke. *Damn, not now, Jase. Not in front of Neil.*

Neil reached out and took my hand. Despite their incessant shaking, he still had those enormously powerful, soft hands. As I had so many times before, I took comfort in his touch. Except this time, I wasn't the little boy that he had met all of those years ago. Nor was I the young teenager who would have done anything to please him. I wasn't even the young man who had rowed loyally for him in Seoul. I had grown up. I was now my own person and I had just achieved something that Neil had many times before me. And, for the first time in my life, I felt as though I was talking to him as another man—and that felt right.

I couldn't talk anymore so I just put my arms around Neil and held him. "I love you, Neil."

As best he could, he was able to get an arm around me. "Me too, Jase."

It felt so good to have acknowledged Neil for everything he had done for me. Aside from my dad, no other man had influenced me as much as Neil had in my lifetime. Sure, we had had our moments that one summer, but in many ways that was simply the nature of the beast rearing its ugly head. It was who we were. It was what made us love competing. After these past nine months, I had a better understanding of Neil's sometimes-abrasive ways. His attention to detail, his unwavering commitment to perfection and his refusal to give up were the reasons we had not only survived the year, but had done so achieving our ultimate performance.

It was undoubtedly a full-circle moment for me. To have come back as a coach and to share all of the lessons, all of the stories and all of the success that I had experienced as result of Neil and rowing—it felt like nothing I had ever felt or achieved before. It was, without question, the highlight of my rowing career.

I returned to the dock alone to wait for my crew. As I waited, some of the members of the Vancouver College crew came down to get their blades.

As they went by, one of them walked over to me with his hand outstretched. "Hey, Coach, congratulations." I reached out my hand to except his gesture, but just before our hands met he pulled his back and gave me the finger. "Fuck you, asshole!"

His teammates came running back to grab him. "Sorry about that, sir. He's just being an idiot."

"No problem. Don't worry about it," I answered, although I was taken aback by what that young Vancouver College athlete had said. The more I thought about it, the more I realized that, sure, most people would've considered what he had done rude and unsportsmanlike, and maybe he was an asshole for saying it to my face, but he really was no different than I had been at his age. When I was 16, I hated the coaches of the other crews too. In fact, in 1982, when we lost to Brentwood in the final, I was thinking the same thing about Tony Carr. I was equally mad and frustrated, but my social graces prevented me from saying it to Tony's face. This young rower had simply learned exactly what I had learned when I was his age—that losing was wrong and that you should be furious with yourself and hate your competitors for beating you. I really couldn't blame him. He was simply behaving the way he thought was right and appropriate.

My quiet moment of reflection was broken by the sound of my crew making its way to the dock. I loved that sound, eight oars cracking through the surface of the water in perfect unison. Magic.

I had told myself that, regardless of the outcome in the final of the eight, I was going to have these guys go for an extended row together. When I had won this race as a teenager, I hated that our row back to the dock from the grandstand was only four or five minutes long. I wanted that row to go on forever. The guys I rowed with were my best friends. I had rowed with some of them for four years—I wanted to savour that moment. I wanted my Shawnigan crew to have that opportunity and some quiet time to process what they had just accomplished.

As they took their last stroke, I eagerly grabbed an oar and began to pull them into the dock. Excited as I was, I couldn't wait to hear what they had to say about the row. "So how was that?" To my surprise, there wasn't one word from any of them. Thinking that they hadn't heard me, I repeated myself a little louder this time. "How was that? What was that like?" Again, not a single reply. With the boat now stopped at the dock and all of them undoing their shoes, I looked more closely at each of them to see why no one was talking. Instantly, it became clear. They were all crying, some of them sobbing uncontrollably.

I stood back and watched them get out of the boat. Immediately, they began to hug one another. With tears running down their faces, they told each other how much they loved one another. For me, it was quite a moment. But amid their heartfelt display of emotion, what struck me was that, even as their coach, the one who had led them through this year, I had completely underestimated what these young boys had been through over the past nine months.

Once composed, we gathered together.

"As I mentioned earlier," I began, "I can't tell you how proud I am of each of you. What you accomplished here today is truly astounding. To have the race that the four did and then come back less then four hours later and do it again like that—it's unbelievable. I had someone come up to me while I was walking down here and tell me that they think your time is a high school world record." Their eyes lit up. "Imagine if you had been fresh! Regardless, what it took to pull off that performance is a testament to what kind of individuals you are and what kind of a crew you are. So, congratulations. Now, before we head up to the trailer, as I just found out—which I'll tell you about later—there are a few crews who aren't too thrilled about you winning. As we've been saying all year long—'if you lose, say nothing; if you win, say less'—keep in mind that we'll have plenty of opportunity to celebrate when we get back to Brock. Enjoy the moment but respect the guys who you've just beaten. Okay, Tay, take 'em up."

With that, the boat was out of the water, resting on their shoulders and making its way back to the trailer, with me following a few feet behind. Looking at the ground as I walked I noticed out of the corner of my eye that someone had stepped into my path. I looked up to see my mom's beaming smile. She gave me a big hug and then grabbed me on both sides of my face and looked right into my eyes. "You did it. You did it, Jason. I'm so proud of you."

There's a place inside every man that only his mother can access. That's because they created it. A place so honest, so vulnerable, that we lose the ability to go there as we grow older. It's not necessarily our fault. It's what we're taught—big boys don't show emotion. We certainly never show signs of being vulnerable, no matter how honest that experience may be for us. With her few short words and her warm embrace, Mom untied that bag and let me experience what today truly meant to me. Secure in the arms of my mom I was undone. The pressure and stress that I had felt going into that regatta were gone and now I felt safe to release them.

On her heels was my dad. "Congratulations, Son. Gosh, that was terrific." Dad, the proud and traditional look-'em-in-the-eye-with-a-firm-handshake kind of a guy, laughed as I gave him a big hug.

When I caught up to my crew, they had already put the boat down on stretchers and were beginning to take it apart. The guys from Hudson Boat Works were there assisting them. They had a long drive ahead of them and they wanted to get going. With the boat de-rigged and loaded onto the trailer, they were away. Our loaner had been good to us—it had been the perfect chariot.

With their families and the other crews now arriving back at the Island, I wanted to have one last chance to speak with my crew. As we gathered together, I was amazed that some of them were still emotional, still crying, still processing the events of the day and the many days and months leading up to it. I reminded them of their incredible accomplishment and of keeping some perspective when celebrating in front of the other crews. More than anything I wanted them to know how much the year had meant to me. I thanked them for the opportunity to coach them. I explained that playing a role in their experience at an event that I had experienced at their age meant the world to me. On that final note we began to joke around. The teasing and insults returned just as they had in the months leading up to this day. On the surface, nothing had really changed, but I believed that deep down every one of us had changed forever.

ABOUT THE AUTHOR

Jason Dorland, former Olympic, Commonwealth Games and World Championship rower, coached the Shawnigan Lake School senior boys' rowing crew to four national championships and an unofficial high school world record time, becoming the first person to win the coveted Calder Cleland Memorial Trophy as an athlete and as a coach.

Jason Dorland was born and raised in St. Catharines, Ontario, where he attended Ridley College and began his rowing career. From there, he accepted a rowing scholarship to Syracuse University for two years before transferring to the University of Victoria and training with the Canadian National Team.

A graduate of the Emily Carr Institute of Art + Design in Vancouver, Jason is a designer, keynote presenter (www.jasondorland.com) and author. He lives with his wife Robyn (www.robynmeagher.com) and family in St. Catharines, Ontario, where he is Director of Rowing at Ridley College (www.ridleyrowing.com). He is also the co-founder, co-owner and creative director of an organic and natural food company, Left Coast Naturals (www.leftcoastnaturals.com).